BOON ISLAND

Plate 2

Boon Island

A
CHART
of The
GULF STREAM

James Poupard, Sculp.

BOON ISLAND

A True Story of Mutiny, Shipwreck, and Cannibalism

ANDREW VIETZE
STEPHEN ERICKSON

Guilford, Connecticut

To buy books in quantity for corporate use
or incentives, call **(800) 962-0973**
or e-mail **premiums@GlobePequot.com**.

Project editor: David Legere
Text design: Sheryl P. Kober
Layout: Sue Murray

Library of Congress Cataloging-in-Publication Data is available on file.

ISBN 978-0-7627-7752-5

Printed in the United States of America

10 9 8 7 6 5 4 3 2 1

Contents

Preface

Last December marked the tricentennial of the horrors of Boon Island. In the three centuries since the *Nottingham Galley* careened into the ledges of the cursed isle, leaving fourteen men to freeze and turn into savages, no writer has ever written a history of the event—at least not at book length. And it's one of the world's greatest tales of survival, a story just begging to be told, full of blood and heart, drama and trauma. This grisly episode has been chronicled in essays, book chapters, academic papers, magazine stories, museum exhibits, and even a couple of fiction-alized accounts—and they so often get it wrong. But no one has ever explored in-depth exactly what happened on that rock six miles off the coast of York—and why.

And then there were two.

I had just finished a piece about the wreck of the *Nottingham Galley* for *Down East: The Magazine of Maine* and was signing a book contract to extend it into a full-length manuscript when I discovered I was not alone on the island. Doing my research, I happened upon an article in the *New England Quarterly* that hinted I'd have some competition. The byline mentioned that the story was from a book-length manuscript on the sub-ject by Portsmouth historian Stephen Erickson. We met and decided the best tack would be to combine our efforts, and the result is the book in your hands. I'd like to thank Stephen for his patience in this process.

I'd also like to thank my editor, Erin Turner, for her enthusiasm for the project, and agent, Russ Galen, for his sage advice.

My parents, as ever, for their steadfast support.

And my wife, Lisa, and my two boys, Gus and Leo—because I realize life with a writer/ranger can sometimes be its own survival epic.

—Andrew Vietze

I ALWAYS THINK OF THE BOON ISLAND CASTAWAYS AROUND THE WINTER holidays, after the temperature outside my house in Portsmouth, New Hampshire, has grown frigid. The colder it is, the more they are on my mind. Sometimes I step outside to be coatless in the winter breeze like they were. I try to imagine what it must have been like. But of course I can't. Thankfully I will never know what it is to lie stranded, hopeless, freezing, and starving on a barren rock out in the ocean. Perhaps I walk a few paces as the ice crunches underfoot before retreating back inside to a warmth they could only imagine in their desperate fantasies.

In an odd coincidence, my ancestor, Samuel Weeks, had just completed his term as Portsmouth Selectman when the survivors of the wreck of the *Nottingham Galley* were brought into town, on January 4, 1711. Weeks must have met and known them. Can a memory be passed down subconsciously through the generations? It seems irrational to think so, but I am a little superstitious about this horrible and mysterious story. During the course of my research, I felt some of the victims of the ill-fated ship's company looking over my shoulder, urging me to get the story right, at last.

I believe, for a variety of reasons, that the wreck of the *Nottingham Galley* is one of the most important but least understood—or most misunderstood—episodes in maritime history. The tale touches on so much: survival, reputation, class conflict, the testing of cultural norms, the power of the written and printed word, and historical memory. It was said to be among the most famous shipwreck stories of the early eighteenth century. It was also the subject of twentieth-century novelist Kenneth Roberts's last historical fiction, *Boon Island*.

I am grateful to the *New England Quarterly* and its editor, Linda Smith Rhoads, for publishing my article, "To Obviate a Scandalous Reflection: Revisiting the Wreck of the *Nottingham Galley*." The article led to my fortuitous partnering with veteran writer and coauthor Andy Vietze, who, through his skill and style, has done much to bring this story to life.

A special thanks goes to Evan Lloyd, M.D., who diagnosed the ailments of the Boon Island castaways from a distance of three centuries. I also want to thank Richard Warner, Marcus Rediker, the British Library, the National Archives of the United Kingdom, the Portsmouth Athenaeum, the Portsmouth Public Library, and the Old York Historical Society.

It is said that history is written by the winners. But sometimes even the less fortunate will find their voice and make it heard.

—Stephen Erickson

PROLOGUE

THE CAPTAIN WAS FURIOUS. YET AGAIN, THE MEMBERS OF HIS CREW HAD FLATLY *disobeyed an order. Rather than remove the corpse, as he'd instructed, they'd slept with it. He tied a rope around the body and began to drag it out of the tent. Heaving on the line, the heavy ship's Carpenter at the other end, the Captain felt dizzy and thought he might faint. Due to the fragile state he himself was in, it took all his effort, and still he was unable to do it.*

His "Spirits being still in Ferment," the Captain recruited a volunteer, and between the two of them, "with some difficulty got it out of the tent." The body was at least outside now. It could be brought down over the icy rock to the shore and disposed of later. With all that effort, and all that anger, the Captain needed to lie down himself and so "crept into the tent: again."

No sooner was he inside than "the Men began to request of [him] the dead Body to eat . . ."

The Captain was rendered speechless, for nothing was "so amazingly Shocking as this unexpected Proposal." During his long silence the sailors urged their desires with "irresistible Vehemence."

After much deliberation he stepped outside to do the ugly deed. First, he removed the parts that made the corpse look human. The head—its eyes staring—was severed. The hands were cut off at the wrists. Then the feet at the ankles. The body was disemboweled, and the organs were removed. These parts were carried off to the water's edge and set reverently there to be taken by the sea. Then the Carpenter was flayed, and the skin was removed to the same location. After that it was simple dressage, like a butcher in a shop or a hunter in the field.

He had asked the boatswain to help him hold the body still, but the boatswain was too weak. So he commandeered the gunner. Once the meat was cut into pieces the Captain brought it into the tent. Each man was given a piece of the ship's Carpenter.

To justify the grisly act, the Captain declared: "It is no Sin, since God was pleas'd to take him out of the World, and that we'd not laid violent hands upon him." The men had prevailed upon him "with incessant Prayers and Tears," begging that the task be done. That night most of them ate the macabre meal, but a few refused. This included the Mate, the Boatswain, and one of the seamen . . .

To make the Carpenter's raw flesh more palatable, the men called it "beef." But, as the Captain noted, "this last Precaution was needless since they devoured it in a rapacious Manner, and crav'd greater Quantities than consisted with health, and the Extent of their small Stock."

During the night the Captain had to stand watch over what was left to make sure the men didn't sneak out of the tent like ghouls to feed.

It was a story he would tell for the remainder of his life.

PART I

A Mysterious Shipwreck

Chapter 1

"Boone Island is the forlornest place that can be imagined..."
—CELIA THAXTER, ISLES OF SHOALS, 1870

THE BODY WAS THIN, EMACIATED EVEN. HIS SKIN WAS A WAXY WHITE, marred with ulcers and blackened in places from freezing, eyes stuck in hollow sockets. The corpse had been discovered lying amid the tidal wrack on the long expanse of beach at Wells. Captain Lewis Bane, the coroner of the small town of York, Province of Maine, was summoned and led to the scene through a snowy woods. It was January first, early and cold, and the miles-long stretch of sand was windswept and desolate.

Surely this wasn't how Bane wanted to begin the New Year. Rather than a fresh start, it seemed history had found the village again—more death. Residents of York—fewer than 120 of them now—had been warring with the native Abenakis intermittently for the past thirty-five years and had barely held on. Hundreds and hundreds of Banes's neighbors, friends, and family—from southern Maine and throughout the small adjacent colony of New Hampshire—had been killed, wounded, or captured in raids on their settlements or picked off one by one in fields and forests. The region's English colonists always had to use caution when they ventured out from the relative safety of their garrison houses, and the party of men who led the coroner through narrow trails to the beach most certainly came with muskets in hand. The Indians might be watching from the trees.

If the Indians were there, waiting in ambush, they too were armed with muskets supplied by the French. The Abenakis had thrown in their lot with the great native leader of the Wampanoags, King Phillip, in 1675.

And they found themselves drawn into a series of imperial wars, working in league with the French of Quebec. The colonists liked to name these global conflicts after their own English monarchs—perhaps it was a kind of political statement, subconscious or not. They called this one with the French and Indians Queen Anne's War, but it would be known as the War of Spanish Succession in Europe.

Few places in the world seemed farther from the machinations of a European court than the coast of Maine in 1711, a wilderness no-man's land dividing English America from French Canada. To the locals it was a mostly empty battleground over which warring parties traveled, and women and children hostages were carried away to be ransomed back again later. Bane's home of York occupied a place on the very edge of English civilization.

And indeed few places had suffered more than York. On a cold January day in 1692, the Abenakis and their French officers had slaughtered one hundred settlers and taken eighty more prisoners during the Candlemas Massacre, forcing the survivors on a grueling march to Canada. While such large-scale attacks were largely over, settlers still risked capture or worse every time they went out to visit a neighbor. The English who lived along in the woods north of the Piscataqua River were a people hardened by war, and Captain Lewis Bane, thirty-nine, owner of timberlands, prominent citizen, and county coroner, was a man accustomed to gruesome sights.

Here was yet another. Bane knelt and looked the dead man over. Had the Indians struck again? It had to be considered. The evidence before the coroner, however, suggested otherwise. There was no sign of struggle or violence. No blood or blunt-force trauma was evident, and the man's scalp was intact. His skin was pocked with chilblains—sores that came about as a result of freezing. But the biggest clue lay on the beach a couple hundred yards away. There Bane noticed a primitive raft, crudely put together from ships tackle. Clearly the man had been on a short journey—this was not the sort of craft anyone would choose to navigate the Gulf of Maine in winter—and had washed ashore. A gaunt body. A raft. A lifelong resident of this southern Maine community, Lewis Bane knew what that meant.

4

The coroner looked up and out to the horizon, on which sat a sliver of gray barely rising above the brine in the distance, a narrow band of rock separating sea from sky. And it had a reputation.

Bane turned and hurried off the beach. He traveled the eleven miles south through the frozen woods to Cape Neddick, a fishing hamlet on the small tidal river of the same name. There he found John Stover, a fisherman who owned a small work boat with a single sail known as a shallop. The coroner commandeered both Stover and his shallop to set out in search of signs of a wreck.

From a line of local fisherman, Stover must have thought this a dubious exercise. Putting out to sea in winter was always a treacherous proposition, and in this case, there had been no reports of any local vessels going missing, and most European seamen knew better than to cross the North Atlantic this time of year. No cannon fire had been heard, indicating a naval engagement with the French or even a signal of distress from a sinking ship. No smoke had been spotted above the islands, and without fire, what were the chances of finding anyone alive on an island in the Gulf of Maine in January?

Still, Bane and Stover were able to convince three others to set sail immediately. It was still morning when they got underway, pushing off from Cape Neddick and following the narrow salt river out to the open sea. The sails of their small shallop filled, and they cleared the harbor and set a course due east, rising and falling on the chop. Their boat was fairly ideal for the Maine coast, an oak-framed vessel with a pine hull and central mast. A shallow draft and the ability to use oars made it able to navigate no matter the weather. But no one liked heading out on days like this.

Six miles offshore was a lonely rock called Boon Island. A tiny isle bereft of vegetation, it was surrounded by ledges that reached out like the tentacles of a kraken, and it was the last resting place of several ships. The island made it on to nautical charts, in fact, thanks to an English merchant vessel called the *Increase*, which slammed on to it in July 1682 in a thick fog during a spring storm. Legend has it that her four-man crew lived off fish and bird's eggs for thirty days until one day they spotted smoke rising from Mount Agamenticus, a hill a few miles from the coast, where the Abenakis were said to be engaged in a religious ritual. The stranded men built a signal fire in response, which the Indians interpreted as a sign from the Great Spirit calling them to the Island. They immediately flew to their canoes and made for the rock, where they found the stranded men. Of course, that was back when relations with the Abenaki were more amicable. The island was then considered a "boon" from God.

Another story claims Boon Island took its very name from the scuttling of ships. So many vessels were said to have foundered there that fishermen left a cache of food on the island—a "boon" for castaways. It might have come from a fisherman named Boone or, more ominously, was a misspelling of *Bone,* which seems darkly appropriate for such a cursed piece of rock.

Stover and his men focused their attention on the isle ahead as it rose slowly up out of the waves. Rectangular in shape, Boon Island is roughly 700 feet long and 300 feet at its widest point at low tide. At high tide much of the island is inundated, reducing its length to as little as 150 feet. The tallest crags atop it stick their heads just 15 feet above sea level, meaning that in storms the whole island can be washed over. It is a barren, desolate rock where nothing can live.

During their hour-long crossing, something bright and white atop the isle caught the eyes of Stover, Bane, and the others. The men maneuvered in slowly, aware of the rocks that lurked just beneath the surface, jagged points that reached out even for boats with little draft, like the shallop. As they drew in closer, they were astonished to spot panels of sailcloth flapping in the winter wind, a cruel and feeble shelter against the brutalities of a North Atlantic winter. Standing outside it, they observed three men, as insubstantial as phantoms, frantically waving. The New England fishermen were dumbfounded. Against all odds shipwreck survivors were alive on Boon Island.

Gesturing and shouting and jumping up and down, the castaways urged their rescuers in to fetch them off the rock. Stover, though, was cautious. The surf was high and the ledges threatened everywhere—there simply was no good place to land. The seasoned sailor decided to drop anchor where he was—about a hundred yards away. He waited there until high tide, when the water would be smoother and there would be more clearance over the hazards below.

When high tide finally flooded in around noon, Stover pulled anchor and followed the directions of one of the castaways to a safe place just off the island. From there the rescue party could shout back and forth to the stranded sailors, who were dangerously thin, sporting long unruly beards, and wearing little, despite the winter temperatures. The shipwrecked men looked much like the man Bane had seen on the beach that morning—wraithlike, without overcoats, the clothing they had in tatters—little to cover their scant human frames except sores and frostbite.

The castaways told the fishermen that there were ten of them left and they'd survived more than three weeks since their ship, the English merchant vessel *Nottingham Galley,* went aground on December 11, during a fierce winter storm. They'd abandoned ship with virtually nothing to help them withstand the ravages of the season, living on the rock with no fire, only a couple of small cheeses for food, and just their raggedy sailcloth tent to protect them from the elements. Two of their comrades had died of exposure and two had left on a raft to get help, never to be seen again.

This, of course, accounted for the body on the beach.

One of the men identified himself as John Deane, captain of the *Nottingham Galley,* and he begged Bane and the fishermen to attempt an evacuation. Captain Deane was ready to be pulled through the waves by rope and buoy if one could be thrown to him. Stover and his men understood the madness in this idea, given the temperatures of the water off Maine this time of year—five or six degrees above freezing—and the frail condition of the captain. But they also realized the gravity of the situation.

Aboard the shallop was a small canoe, which one of the rescuers agreed to take ashore. He would test the waters, so to speak, and see if it would be possible, given the blustery conditions, to get the men safely off the rock. A pall was falling across the skies, and the seas were beginning to heave. No one wanted a repeat of the event that had landed the men there in the first place. The Maine fisherman dropped his canoe into the choppy water, eased himself aboard, and negotiated the waves and rocks with difficulty, but at last made shore.

What the Cape Neddick fisherman saw when he was able to stand on Boon Island rendered him speechless. He was horrified by the captain's "thin and meagre Aspect"—and Deane was one of the healthiest survivors. The captain led the shocked rescuer to the tent, sailcloth luffing in the growing breeze, and pulled the flap open to reveal the other seven men. They were lying huddled together on the rocky ground, and the sight and smell of them repulsed the rescuers' senses. As Deane observed: "He was perfectly affrighted at the Ghastly Figure of so many dismal Objects, with long Beards, nothing but skin and bone; wild staring Eyes, and Countenances, fierce, barbarous, unwash'd and infected with Human gore."

Some of the shipwreck victims crawled toward their savior, gathered around him, clutching his ankles with their swollen, frostbitten hands and sobbing. Bane, Stover, and their small crew had moved with such haste—or perhaps with no serious expectation of finding anyone alive—that they'd neglected to bring any food, so the fisherman had nothing to offer. Instead he provided the only consolation he could—he built a fire right inside the tent.

The rescuers decided the evacuation would begin not with the most infirm but the most able. Deane followed the fisherman back to his canoe and climbed in with him, pushing off toward the shallop. The two men paddled with all their strength, but the waves drove the little craft against a rock and tipped it over, leaving the pair stumbling through frigid water up to their chests. The cold of the water forced the air out of their lungs and held them there as if frozen in place. The wind bit at whatever flesh remained above the sea.

Still extremely weak, Deane "had a very narrow escape from drowning," as he recalled later. Any physical exertion was difficult for him, but the two men managed to haul themselves back onto the island, where they stood soaking wet in the chilling air. Obviously, this wasn't going to work. Most of the shipwrecked men were in far worse shape than their captain, confined to the tent and too sick to risk further exposure, too weak to swim if they capsized. (Perhaps this is what Deane was thinking selecting himself to be rescued first.)

The fisherman retrieved the canoe and, now alone, laboriously made his way back through the rolling seas and past the hateful ledges out to Stover's shallop. Stover yelled to the castaways that he'd return with help as soon as he possibly could. As the skies above began to blacken with storm clouds, the shallop pulled away from the crew of the *Nottingham Galley*'s island prison, leaving the stranded men stranded still.

Frustrated that they could do no more, Stover and the rest of the rescue party turned their sailboat for home, making plans to speed south to the larger city of Portsmouth as soon as they landed to alert the authorities there. As the men talked, the seas began to buffet their small vessel. The storm they'd seen organizing overhead suddenly overtook them, and waves pitched their boat around as if it were a piece of weightless wood.

Waves and spray penetrated clothing to the skin and filled up the craft's relatively shallow hull, as wave after wave after wave tossed the little boat and crashed over its sides. There was no room on the boat to pace to keep warm. But there was plenty of opportunity for exercise, nonetheless, for the men aboard were forced to bail for their lives in a life-threatening battle against the rising water, which sloshed around, numbing their feet beyond feeling.

Would Boon Island claim yet another vessel?

By the time the shallop approached the mainland, the storm was raging and Stover didn't dare attempt a landing for fear of being dashed upon the rocks. A ship's best chance in a storm—to avoid a fate similar to that of the *Nottingham Galley*—is to stay out to sea and ride it out. The men aboard Stover's shallop didn't have that kind of time; they could only stay out for so long before risking death from the cold. Hours passed, and the waves hammered relentlessly as the dark clouds blackened into night. The storm refused to abate. If anything it intensified. Without food the men aboard Stover's boat lost strength, so that the bailing became less vigorous, and the lack of movement increased the threat of hypothermia. One way or another they had to get ashore, rocks or no rocks.

On the mainland the scattered community of settlers who lived around York worried and watched the coast. Closely knit, intermarried, and forced together still more than usual in these dangerous times, hundreds of people had some connection—a father, a brother, a cousin, or a friend—with the men on the shallop. The leaders of the community, like Bane himself, carried a special burden for the safety of the fisherman—they had sent these men out into danger on official business.

Eyes straining through the wintery precipitation, someone by some miracle caught sight of them making their way for the shore. The shallop would be dashed against the rocks. They would need help getting out of the water. Word went out: Stover and his men were coming in.

But, as one observer noted: "The next morning early the Shallope by the Violence of the weather was drove on shore and cast away."

Chapter 2

THREE DAYS LATER, WHEN THE CASTAWAYS FINALLY CAME ASHORE TO the safety of the mainland, Captain John Deane was like something from a nightmare. He looked like he'd just stepped out of a casket, his hair wild and stringy, his skin pocked with sores, his frame shockingly bony. Mostly, though, it was the eyes, which were wide with unconstrained glee. As soon as the canoe bearing him docked, on the Piscataqua River in Kittery, Province of Maine, just downstream from Portsmouth, New Hampshire, the captain leaped from the boat and darted across the lawn of a local home. It was well after dark—about 8 p.m.—and he had two things on his mind.

Exuding a desperate energy, Deane burst into the house, where he found the matriarch home with her children. The sailor's appearance was "to the terrible Affrightment of the Gentlewoman and her Children, who took the first Opportunity to make a fair Escape." The captain then, "unmercifully hungry," took the occasion to head to the kitchen to "rumage the Pot." He found some beef and some turnips. "Resolving thereupon to stand Cook for once," Deane spread his findings on the table and began to eat. He had already "secured some small portion in his Belly" when the men who had paddled him ashore arrived and "unacceptably restrained him from eating any more at that time."

This was no random home invasion, however. Deane was the invited guest of Captain Jethro Furber, a Portsmouth shipmaster whom he knew from the small world of North Atlantic trade. Furber and Captain William Long, an Englishman recently arrived, like Deane himself, had put together a fleet of sloops to rescue the castaways on Boon Island as soon as they could safely do so. Word had come from York of the plight of the crew of the *Nottingham Galley*, but evacuation had been impossible for several days. The storm that had overtaken Lewis Bane, John Stover, and their crew had lingered, making conditions simply too dangerous to venture out on the Gulf of Maine. Stover, Bane, and their fishermen friends had barely survived their own shipwreck; when they finally made it to shore, they made good on their promise to send help.

Furber and Long pushed off from Portsmouth in a fleet of four sloops almost as soon as the skies broke on the morning of January 4. As they neared the island, the rescuers could see smoke rising from a hole in the center of the makeshift tent. Like Stover had before them, the local sailors drew their vessels as close as they dared and then launched a large canoe—this one more seaworthy than Stover's—to transport the survivors. Deane and one or two others were able to walk under their own power, but some "strong Men, brought the rest, two or three at a time, most of them on their backs from the tent to the canoe, though none of them were free of vermin."

This time—to the great joy of the castaways—the mission was a success, and the men of the *Nottingham Galley* finally realized the deliverance for which they'd been praying. Once safely aboard the sloops, each of the evacuees was given a dram of rum and then some bread, as the Captain recalled. The sudden introduction of food and alcohol to their shrunken stomachs—along with the motion of the waves—made most of them violently ill. This was intentional on the part of their rescuers. Such a purging was thought necessary to cleanse their digestive systems. Afterward they were kept on a strict and gradual diet to allow the healing of their insides to begin. Deane's recovery was to take place at his friend Furber's home, and the large canoe was dropped overboard when they reached the mouth of the Piscataqua River to carry Deane and the especially sickly gentleman survivor, Miles Whitworth, to the shore near Furber's house. There Deane bolted from the boat and made his mad dash for the kitchen. After seeing to the safety of Whitworth, the men chased after the captain and had to hold him back to keep him from gorging himself, which can be fatal after a prolonged period of starvation.

With the incoming tide the flotilla carrying the remaining castaways turned up into the Piscataqua River, part of an estuary that empties the Great Bay, twelve miles inland. On the port side they passed the relatively well-settled island of New Castle, on which sat the waterway's only defense, the diminutive Fort William and Mary, from which a few cannons defiantly poked out. The survivors sailed on past many fishing shallops tied up or hauled on shore, and then made for Portsmouth.

Word of the horror on Boon Island had spread quickly through the region's largest town, and a small crowd gathered to witness the arrival of the sloops bearing the skeletal crew of the *Nottingham Galley*. The people of Portsmouth had been curious about the fate of the English sailors ever since an express rider arrived from York with news that another ship had gone aground on Boon Island. The accursed rock lay only fifteen miles away, beyond the archipelago known as the Isles of Shoals, and any captain worth his sea legs knew of the hazards that lie under the sea there.

Shipwrecks and seafaring accidents were nothing new to the roughly two thousand people of Portsmouth. The men and women who lived in the rows of unpainted, postmediaeval homes understood the Atlantic as well as any could. Salt air nipped at their gables and gambrel roofs, and most eked out their livelihood from the sea in one way or another. The town sat two miles from the open ocean—as the seagull flew—astride the Piscataqua, which rose and fell as many as twelve feet with the swings of the tide. This tidal action—and a rip current as fast as any navigable river in North America—kept the harbor from freezing over, as so many others did in New England, which in turn kept the city in business all winter long. (The muscular underwater pull gave the river its name—*Piscataqua* is a native word for "river of strong currents.")

Originally named Strawbery Banke for the fruit growing along the shore, Portsmouth was an unlikely place for a port—the anchorage was limited and the river approaching was crowded with islands. But the town was advantageously located between two tidal ponds, one to its north and one to its south. Near the intersections of each pond and the Piscataqua River, tide-powered gristmills ground wheat and corn to help provide the town with vital sustenance. The ponds were also useful for defense, because they provided a natural moat on the two sides perpendicular to the river. A stockade fence that ran between the two bounded Portsmouth to the west.

The sickly, cold-ravaged sailors of the *Nottingham Galley* were landed into a town showing many signs of war. It was crowded with refugees from more exposed settlements, including idle men looking for work. The many sawmills located along the region's small rivers and streams were frequently quieted by the war, and agriculture, too, was set back due to the threat of Indian attack. Area fishermen plied their trade under the constant danger of being taken by French privateers operating out of Canada.

A few old garrison houses, with their overhanging second floors, still stood inside the town, a reminder that the zone of safety from Indian attack was, over the course of decades, slowly being pushed back. Portsmouth's poor lived crowded into dark, earth-fast homes, while a few wealthy merchants were already well on their way to establishing a colonial oligarchy. A solid middle class of artisans and tradesmen, though now struggling, occupied the social and physical spaces in between.

When the sloops docked, a mixture of citizens, from indigent to affluent, watched as the castaways were unloaded like cargo and carried over Portsmouth's frozen, muddied, and snow-covered streets to a nearby tavern, to lie by a precious fire, eat some morsels of food, and begin their long recoveries. The nursing began immediately.

Though he was reduced to skin and bone, Deane considered himself otherwise in "perfect Health." Safe and warm in Furber's home, Deane wasted no time putting pen to paper, drawing up documents for his legal defense. After a merchant vessel was lost at sea through some natural disaster beyond the control of the captain and crew, the ship's commander was required to draw up a "protest," a legal brief describing the incident. As soon as Deane could hold a quill, he began drafting a written account of the circumstances that brought his ship to bear on Boon Island. Deane's original written protest doesn't survive but likely included only the story of the ship hitting the island and excluded what happened on the island afterward.

Protests were an obligation of the captain—they were used to absolve him and his crew of wrongdoing—but Deane seemed particularly obsessed with his, writing it before he'd seen to his own health or the health of his men. He spent several days getting the wording of the document just right, and when he finished he took it over to the tavern where his men were recovering. He wanted to get the ranking members of the crew—the first mate and boatswain—to sign off on his story as soon as possible. His haste and single-mindedness must have struck some in Portsmouth as odd.

What had happened out there?

The scene at the tavern was grim. A Doctor Packer, who local authorities had assigned to look after the survivors, had been kept busy amputating fingers and toes. Every man in the crew had lost at least one digit. Remarkably only the ships' boy had lost more than that—half his foot was cut away. Most were still very sick and unable to stir from their beds when Deane arrived. Without much ado he secured the signature of his first mate, who was gripped by fever, too ill to read or concentrate on the document. The boatswain, however, refused to give the captain his approval. What was said between them is lost to history. But what happened next isn't: The captain simply dubbed one of the other sailors boatswain on the spot and had him sign instead.

The original boatswain's refusal to cooperate—harsh words were spoken and accusations were made—only deepened the sense of intrigue surrounding the ship and its castaways. No one was more curious about the story than the great Puritan minister, Cotton Mather, who asked friends in Portsmouth repeatedly for details. The theology of the day assumed that anything bad that happened to people—such as a shipwreck—was a result of God's judgment. Puritans like Mather were especially keen on this notion, and the reverend had already weaved the news of the wreck into one of his Thursday sermons down in Boston, apparently attracting much attention. Mather made reference to men "over-run with Ulcers," "starving to Death," and "Breaking on the Rock," hoping to exploit public interest in the terrifying event to impress upon people, and particularly sailors, the power of God's wrath and the potential for His mercy. He intended to publish the sermon, but he wanted as much information as he could get, so he sent a letter to his old friend Samuel Penhallow, a Portsmouth magistrate, asking for an account of "the astonishing Example of outrageous wickedness among the strangers lately broke into your Neighborhood." Mather wanted to be the one to break the story, so he pressed Penhallow for an "Expressive and Punctual Relation of the horrid Matter, and such as one, as being well attested, may be Relied upon."

"The Least material Mistake," he added, "may be a great Inconvenience . . . Write me then this week, a Letter that shall give me the Story with all the circumstances, which you think proper to have Exposed unto the World." Little did he know just how outrageous and wicked the story was.

Deane would tell Mather—and the world—his tale. He wanted it heard—and he wanted it told his way.

PART II

THE CAPTAIN'S STORY

Chapter 3

IT WAS AN ACCIDENT. A MINOR NAVIGATIONAL ERROR MADE ON THE sort of hell's-fury night that all sailors dread. The cold North Atlantic threw everything it had at the *Nottingham Galley* on the evening of December 11, 1710. A gale drove the English merchant vessel through a dark tunnel of hail and rain and snow. The seas heaved all around, waves rising into mountains. Between the blackness of the evening and the low-lying clouds, visibility was limited to little more than the boat's own decks and rigging. As Captain John Deane explained, it was a good night for wrecking a ship.

At 120 tons, the *Nottingham Galley* was about the smallest vessel anyone would want for a transatlantic crossing. Fifty feet in length and twelve foot abeam, give or take, with the wide-open decks and tall stern that characterized the galley, she had a shoal-form hull, flattened out at the bottom, which was useful in shallow waters, or when being rowed in dead-calm seas.

On that particular night, the seas were anything but calm, and her hull was a liability. She was tossed about like a leaf on a breeze.

Huge swells lifted the ship and then rolled heavily underneath her, allowing her to plunge nauseatingly down. The small vessel recovered her buoyancy much slower than boats with more conventionally shaped hulls, leaving her perilously positioned up on her beam end every few seconds and in danger of capsizing. After righting herself, she'd lift back up on the waves and plunge back down. On this night, she rocked up and down. And up and down. For hours on end.

At the same time, powerful wind gusts yanked demonically at the light sail the ship was carrying, jerking hard at the rigging. The temperature hovered around freezing as sheets of rain, snow, and ice continued to blow out of the northeast, lashing the decks and stinging the faces of the men struggling to work on their pitching platform. One sailor of the time noted that working conditions deteriorated as weather conditions did. When water froze, it could make the "smallest rope in the ship as big as one's arm and the (ropes) so cold and slippery and sharp that they would cut our hands when hauling upon them." This was one of those nights.

Deane and his thirteen-man crew had been fighting the weather ever since they shoved off at Killybags, Ireland, eleven weeks earlier bound for Boston with a load of cordage and cheese. December was not the time of year to be on the North Atlantic.

Thirty-one-year-old Deane was aware of the dangers of the crossing, but with risk came opportunity. And the captain, an experienced mariner, was a man of many ambitions. Quite aside from the hazards of a cold-weather journey, it was wartime, with French privateers hunting the Atlantic. If an early winter squall didn't get you, a cruising corsair might well do so. But there was money to made through the cordage in the *Nottingham Galley*'s hold if Deane could get it to its destination. The crossing was meant to happen before December, but, as Deane complained, "contrary winds and bad weather" had slowed their progress. And now this. The *Nottingham Galley* was caught in a classic nor'easter.

The seas between Europe and North America were notoriously treacherous in winter, when arctic Labrador currents waged their own little war against the warmer waters of the Gulf Stream, creating hurricane-like nor'easters. During these powerful storms seas can swell as high as thirty or forty feet and wind can blow fifty miles an hour or more, typically not as strong as those of its southern cousin—but nor'easters tend to live longer and spread farther than hurricanes. A nor'easter can last up to a week if it stalls off the coast, and when it does it can dump mammoth amounts of precipitation over a large region before the prevailing winds encourage it to move along. Though these violent storms can happen any time of year, they're typically associated with winter. And no other region of the world provides the conditions for nor'easters quite like the New England coast.

With the wind blowing fiercely, the captain stood on deck trying to peer through the murk. The clouds and fog made it practically impossible to navigate—they'd been uncertain exactly where they were for more than a week. But on they pushed toward Massachusetts Bay. This night was the worst they'd seen, and Deane ordered most of the ship's sails taken in. In spite of the heavy winds and heaving seas—and the fact that he could hardly see beyond the bowsprit—the *Nottingham Galley* continued on, still carrying its foresail and top mainsail. Sailing in such brutal conditions was a risk-laden proposition, and rough weather almost always meant reducing sail. Most galleys were ship rigged, meaning that they had three masts, with two or three square sails each. In addition, the *Nottingham Galley* carried a spritsail on the bowsprit and almost certainly two or more jibs, staysails, and studding sails. Men scurried about lashing sails to yardarms.

The high seas, gale-force winds, and impenetrable fog made it an all-hands-on-deck situation. The sailors of the *Nottingham Galley* divided their work and rest time into larboard and starboard watches, and the crew was split up by experience. Thus the first mate and the boatswain, the two most seasoned sailors, supervised alternating watches. Each watch included at least four men, not counting the captain. The two gentleman passengers aboard—Deane's brother, Jasper, and Miles Whitworth, who co-owned the ship with the two Deanes—were not assigned a watch, nor were the ship's cook or carpenter, who had other tasks to mind. Watches required the sailor to be in position for four hours, and they rotated, which meant that no seaman ever got more than four hours of sleep at a stretch. And there were the occasions, like this, when everyone was needed.

On December 11, though, there was one man missing. Captain Deane normally would have left this watch to the first mate, an experienced hand and perhaps the best sailor on board, but Christopher Langman was not feeling well. (As Deane put it, he was "slightly indisposed.") His input would have been invaluable on such a violent night, but he was belowdecks recuperating. So, sometime between 8 and 9 p.m., John Deane decided to have one last look around himself.

The captain walked forward to the bow and did his best to peer through the seamless wall of gray. It was too dark—and the skies were filled with pelting sleet—to see much. But to Deane's "infinite sirprize" he could hear a sound emanating from the blackness ahead, a percussive boom that terrified him, chilling him as much as the freezing winter spray. Above the shriek of the storm came the distinct thud of surf crashing. Even worse was the scene emerging from the clouds in front of him—he could just make out the spray of foam directly in the ship's path. Thundering breakers and frothing sea could only mean one thing—a massive rock pushing up from the depths.

The captain screamed back to the helmsman to turn the ship hard to starboard. Panicking or not hearing well through the gale, the sailor spun the wheel in the opposite direction. It would have been too late to correct their course anyway—turning a vessel the size of the *Nottingham Galley* took time—time they didn't have.

The impact was devastating.

The boat came to a sudden, crunching halt, hitting a ledge with "great violence," as Deane recalled. The *Nottingham Galley* struck with "two vehement thumps upon the rock and a third sea hove the ship along the side of it." Anyone not holding on went flying, dashed from his feet, hitting his head and elbows as he bounced off the deck and slid into walls. As if sensing weakness, the cruel seas began to push the ship over against the rock, frigid brine pouring into the broken hull and towering swells crashing over her bow. The dark was so complete that no one knew what it was exactly that they had hit.

Waves hammered the side of the heavy vessel, each time slamming it further down onto the rock. Winter seas washed over the decks, and the scrambling sailors careened about in chaos. Soon the angle of the ship on the rocks became so great, and the wave action across them so powerful, it was impossible to stand on deck.

"The Sea running very high, and violently beating upon us, laboured the ship so excessively, that we looked every Moment that she would fall to pieces," remembered Deane. The ferocious combination of winds, waves, and water pushed, pulled, and pounded on the side of the *Nottingham Galley* and struck terror into the heart of her company.

"The weather was so thick and Dark," said the captain, "we cou'd not see the Rock, so that we were justly thrown into a Consternation at the sad Prospect of immediately perishing in the Sea."

With the snow, sleet, or freezing rain; the listing and icy deck underfoot; the howl and feel of the wind; the sound of boards scraping and collapsing; the relentless pounding of the ship against the rock; the sight of the furious, foaming, surging ocean; fellow sailors yelling, ordering, crying, or paralyzed with fear, thoughts of home, escape, and death rushed through their minds like the water pouring into the *Nottingham Galley*. Complete sensory overload.

Psychologists call this moment the "period of impact." The normal response is a numbing bewilderment. Most people caught up in disasters—and likely facing death—appear stunned, and they experience impaired reasoning, tunnel vision, and a difficulty expressing emotion. Physically, they are apt to tremble, become nauseous and weak, and possibly defecate. Training and experience can make a huge difference, but many men of the *Nottingham Galley* were rendered useless during this moment of maximum peril.

Not Captain John Deane, as he told people later. He calmly ordered the crew to gather in the main cabin, and when all fourteen members of the ship's company were present, they prayed, "earnestly supplicating Mercy." They not only bowed their heads, but they did so for a few minutes, sheltered from the weather between decks, as the hull scraped along the rocks below, screaming as it dragged. The listing of the vessel continued, and they constantly shifted their stances in order to keep balance, until they found themselves standing on the walls of the cabin.

"Knowing Prayers without Endeavors are vain I order'd all up again, to cut the Masts by the board," Deane said. It was time for action, and the captain meant to have it. Some men, though, ignored his commands, continuing to experience paralysis. "Several sunck so under racks of

Conscience that they were not able to stir." But a number of them resolutely climbed back out into the storm.

The cutting of the ship's masts in a debilitating storm is a time-honored act of desperation. If the situation is dire, masts are "cut by the board" as Deane ordered—chopped right at their bases and felled like trees—to reduce the profile of the ship, improve buoyancy, and decrease the likelihood of capsizing.

In this case the weight of the masts of the *Nottingham Galley* was conspiring with the punishing winds to push the vessel completely over on its side. The little sail they still carried only added to the effect, and if the rigging, spars, and reefed sails were caked with ice, the additional weight posed an even greater threat.

At least one brave crew member climbed the mast to cut away the remaining sails. Others got to work at its base, desperately chopping with axes while trying to keep their footing as the ship heaved and water continued to wash across the deck. Fortunately the wind made quick work of the chore. The masts came crashing down one at a time, with the foremast landing on an unseen ledge.

The mast "Providently falling to the rock," Deane recalled, "I desired some men to try if, by the help of the Masts, they could recover the Shoar, and let us know their safety by their calls to us." Two or three crewmen volunteered, climbing up onto the long mast and crawling out across it. And in so doing they disappeared into the night. "The fierceness of the wind and the roaring of the sea perfectly drowned their Voices," Deane remembered, "and we considered them lost."

As his men were climbing courageously into the unknown, Deane himself went belowdecks to gather items that he thought might be of use—money, papers, brandy, and ammunition. He didn't last long. The *Nottingham Galley* was under enormous stress. Breakers were pounding incessantly on the walls. The hull was dragging on the bottom. The wooden beams of the ship were groaning under the pressure. Deane grabbed his flint and steel and his gunpowder, but as he turned to find the box containing his money, the hull burst at the stern and water came flooding in—"the ship bulging, her decks

24

opened, her back broke, and her beams gave way, so that the stern sunk under water."

The captain bolted for the deck above. "[I] hastened forward," he recalled, "to prevent immediate perishing." Topside, Deane threw off his wig and coat. He paused there, listening for the men who had already gone over the side. Hearing nothing above the banshee winds, he concluded they were lost. He had no other choice but to follow. The ship wouldn't remain above the water for more than a few minutes.

The captain found the slippery foremast pointing out into gloom. Crawling out onto it, he threw himself, with every bit of strength that he had, into the black.

Chapter 4

OF COURSE IT WASN'T SUPPOSED TO HAPPEN THIS WAY. WHEN THE
Nottingham Galley left London on August 7, hopes for a successful voyage
were high. John Deane was an experienced sailor, and he was undoubtedly
excited about being at the helm of his own ship. He and his brother, Jasper, had gone in on this trading venture together, along with their father
and another merchant, Miles Whitworth. They bought a fine vessel, put
together a crew, filled the hold, and were ready to haul sails under the late
summer sun. Jasper held the lion's share of interest in the ship, though
exactly who owned how much of the cargo remains a bit unclear. Besides
Whitworth, and the senior Deane, several other area investors had also
purchased shares.

Jasper was thirty-three, two years older than his brother, and had
spent some time at sea himself—in his will, written in 1705, Jasper lists
his own profession as "mariner." But he didn't have quite the same depth
of experience as John, who according to folklore had made a name for
himself during the early years of the War of the Spanish Succession off
Malaga, Spain. The younger Deane is said to have been among the English fleet that defeated the French there, securing the mouth of the Mediterranean for England for all time.

The owners of the vessel obviously thought enough of John's nautical skills to give him the helm of the *Nottingham Galley*, while Jasper, the
mariner, would serve as supercargo, or director of business dealings, at his
side. The arrangement was an unusual one—subverting the tradition of a
captain who ruled absolutely once at sea—and to work, the brothers had
to come to decisions harmoniously. They'd have to trust one another and

put whatever sibling rivalries they once had aside. Whether or not they were capable of that is another question.

The two Deanes were the sons of Jasper Deane Sr. and Mary Deane of Wilford, England, which lies just across the River Trent from the bustling town of Nottingham, at the time one of the most important municipalities in one of the world's most important countries. Local folklore has it that the Deane family, of a formerly high social status, saw their fortunes fall by 1710, and the senior Jasper Deane invested in the voyage with his sons in the hopes of redeeming his name.

The family's relatively exalted place in the complex social order of English society didn't seem to matter much to John as a boy. The youngster had seen something in the butcher shop that caught his eye, and he had determined that a career carving meat was for him. No doubt his father was horrified at his son's ambition to be a tradesman, and he was probably disappointed further still when John began poaching the king's deer herds—as legend has it—for his meat supply. This put him in the sights of the local constabulary, and it's said that John either ran off to the navy to escape jail time—or was sent by the authorities as an alternative.

How the two brothers came to the decision to buy a ship and partner in the shipping trade is lost to history, but no one aboard the *Nottingham Galley* had more in the balance than Jasper Deane. He owned most of the ship and a significant share of the cargo, investments that constituted a very large percentage of his total wealth, and the risk he took in the venture seems unusually high. Merchant investors of the period tended to remain safe at home and band together in groups or trading companies to minimize the financial risk of any given voyage. Not so for Jasper Deane. Unlike brother John, who was a bachelor at the time, Jasper had a wife and at least one daughter depending on him back in Wilford. And yet he staked his own life and his family's future on a successful voyage across the Atlantic. With so much at risk, he no doubt wanted to personally look after his fortunes. The entire Deane family seems to have concentrated its dwindling family resources, financial and personal, aboard the *Nottingham Galley* in a high-stakes gambit to help reestablish their social position.

For some reason, the wealthy merchant Miles Whitworth, who hailed from Burton Lazars in Leicestershire, about twenty miles south of Nottingham, also decided to make the crossing. In addition to his minor stake in the ship itself, Whitworth presumably also had some small amount of cargo aboard, but he seems more a passenger on the voyage than a trader. Like Jasper, Whitworth was a father—seven children waited for him at home at the time the ship departed London. Why he would choose to risk everything to make an autumn crossing of the Atlantic, with riches and a family at home, remains a mystery.

In the cargo hold of the *Nottingham Galley* was cordage—rope for rigging—that had been brought aboard in London. Made from hemp imported almost exclusively from Russia, rope for anchor and sheet cables was in very high demand, especially during wartime. Large quantities of rope were needed to outfit a single ship, let alone the entire navy and merchant fleet of England. With warships sinking, and new vessels being launched to replace them, the demand created by the war engulfing Europe was extraordinary, and it was difficult to get hemp from Russia through sea lanes choked with both naval vessels and raiding privateers.

Demand for rope and rigging was usually even higher in the colonies. The rope-making industry was slow to take hold in English America because it was labor intensive, and labor in the colonies was notoriously expensive. At least one colony resorted to offering bounties, or subsidies, to support local cordage manufacturing. The Deane family and the other merchant owners of the cordage stowed on the *Nottingham Galley* could have expected a very tidy profit in Boston, if they had gotten there.

A second cargo, this one of butter and cheese, was loaded in Ireland. Dairy products could easily take up the smaller spaces aboard ships not stowed with cordage, and they were much cheaper in Ireland than they were in London. The colonies were a natural market not only for rope and cheese but for all manner of manufactured goods. In the early eighteenth century, North America and the Caribbean holdings of England were still relatively primitive places, full of natural resources and many exports that the British Isles needed—pine masts, furs, tobacco, and sugar—but they had a great need for many imports. Naval stores—like the cordage of the *Nottingham Galley*—received parliamentary bounties or subsidies.

Shipping routes by this time were well defined, and the "mercantil-ist" traditions were well in place. The Navigation Acts in 1650 and 1651 had made it illegal for the colonies to trade with any other nation save Britain—so it was a closed-loop system. The colonists made every effort to circumvent these restrictions, beginning a profitable black market, but they benefited from the law as well, and between 1660 and 1770 the value of colonial trade exploded from 600,000 English pounds to 1,175,000. All of this cargo had to be floated across the sea somehow, and the *Nottingham Galley* was but one ship riding the wave.

Long periods of war often interrupted this growth, however. In time of conflict the cost of trade increased due to higher wages, rising insur-ance rates, and property destroyed or taken at sea. And the ongoing War of Spanish Succession was miserably long. It had been going on since 1702 and would last until 1713.

By the autumn of 1710, when the *Nottingham Galley* sailed, war wea-riness weighed heavily on the nations of Europe. At issue was the ques-tion of who would occupy the vacant throne of Spain after Charles II, who didn't produce a direct heir. One of the claimants was French King Louis XIV's grandson Phillip, whose succession would have united Spain and France and thrown the balance of power in Europe into considerable disarray. Phillip's main rival was Leopold I of Austria, who insisted that Spain remain part of the Hapsburg dynasty and wished to put his own son upon the throne. To check French power, England and Holland had joined the conflict on the side of Austria. Various German states had thrown in their lots with Leopold.

The ensuing war made the always risky business of Atlantic trade more dangerous than usual for merchant shippers. The *Nottingham Galley* might encounter both enemy warships and French privateers, which were terrorizing English ships not just in European waters but off of North America as well. And they'd be sailing into the Atlantic hurricane season, a menace in its own right.

But the Deane brothers and their crew departed London in plenty of time to avoid winter weather, and a military escort, the *Nottingham Galley*'s speed, its ten guns, and its shallow draft offered various forms of protection from the enemy. As Captain Deane and his little vessel weighed anchor on the Thames River in August 1710, a promising voyage began.

If all went according to the stated plan, the *Nottingham Galley* would make the three-thousand-mile journey without incident and arrive in port in six weeks' time, around the end of September.

The best laid plans, of course, are easily foiled by the hands of fate.

Chapter 5

THE MAST JUTTED OUT INTO THE DARK OF NIGHT. CAPTAIN JOHN DEANE clung to it, straddling the stout piece of pine with his legs dangling into the sea. His feet would occasionally touch bottom, but as he crawled out into the blackness, he came to a terrifying point—the long wood beam ended before he reached the safety of the rock. He had no choice but to let go, pushing off into the violent surf. The surging, churning waves tossed him about wildly and he was powerless against them. Deane was "heav'd with such Violence against the craggy Point of the Rock" that it "bruised his Body and tore his Hands miserably."

In desperation, the captain reached out and grabbed at the granite, clutching it for a moment, gasping for breath, but he was unable to hang on as the wave receded, pulling him back with it. Deane became like a breaker himself—"carried off again into the sea"—dashed against the rock then washing back out only to ride the next wave toward safety. He was nearing exhaustion as he tumbled in the surf, swallowing a large quantity of the frigid salt water.

The water was numbing, and he felt his strength fading. The December ocean, of course, was barely above freezing, and the cold drained the Captain's energy. Water temperatures in the Gulf of Maine are in the low forties during the winter, so frigid that simply being immersed feels like being squeezed in a vice. No one can last more than thirty or forty minutes before losing consciousness. Deane was aware of the danger, "preserving the use of his Reason," and knew he didn't have long before he would no longer be able to move and would slip below the surface.

The captain channeled his resources for a final push and hurled himself upward on an incoming wave, grabbing a rock with such desperation that he ripped the flesh and nails right off his fingers. By clinging and clawing his way up the shore, he was able to drag himself "into a place of Security before the next Revolution of the Sea." There he collapsed, coughing, and vomiting seawater.

As he moved a little higher up the shore toward safety, Deane could hear voices emanating from the darkness, and he began to make his way toward them, finding the men who had first climbed out onto the mast. They all continued pushing farther up onto the rock, and in the gloom, stumbled onto the remaining members of the ships' company. Despite the tumult of the weather and the violence of the wreck, the sea had claimed no one. All hands had survived the landing on Boon Island and had made it ashore.

The men of the *Nottingham Galley* were lucky. Deane knew this noting, "with joyfull hearts we return'd humble thanks to Providence for our Deliverance from so eminent a danger." But they were even more fortunate than they may have realized. Maritime historian Peter Earle suggests that on any given voyage during this period, a merchant ship had a 3 to 5 percent chance of foundering. Of the vessels that wrecked, he estimates that some loss of life could be expected in 25 percent of the cases. Of these, all hands perished half of the time. The fatality rate in shipwrecks is statistically not as high as might be imagined, because many wrecks were not especially traumatic events—sometimes vessels simply ran aground on a sandbar—and in most cases there was plenty of time for crews to abandon ship. The other mitigating factor is the extraordinary skill and ingenuity of the average sailor, most of whom knew how to handle a ship or a small lifeboat in a storm, make necessary repairs on the fly, or even construct a life raft out of wreckage. Mariners tended to be tough, hardened, resourceful men who knew how to survive. Still, if shipwrecks in winter storms are considered separately, then fatality rates are considerably higher. Likewise, ships that are driven against rocks tend to rip open and sink quicker, leaving less time for escape. The circumstances of the wreck of the *Nottingham Galley* increased the likelihood of fatality far above the norm. By the odds all of them should have been dead.

The key to survival for the crew was the limited time they spent in the water. They seem to have been in the ocean individually for no more than fifteen minutes, and maybe significantly less. Another local shipwreck, this one a hundred years later on the Isles of Shoals, twelve miles southwest of Boon Island, provides a contrast. Like the *Nottingham Galley*, the Spanish ship *Seguntum* was scuttled in a snowstorm, on the night of January 14, 1813. At that time the Isles of Shoals had a small population, but the tragedy unfolding offshore went completely unnoticed as the residents of the islands slept.

In the morning the fishermen of these small barren islands began to discover bodies. One unfortunate *Seguntum* crewman is said to have collapsed on the stone wall a few steps from the house of Samuel Haley on Smuttynose Island. Thirteen other corpses were found, the final fourteenth recovered in the water on January 21, a whole week after the shipwreck. Given the scattered nature of the dead, and the fact that none survived the night, it is pretty clear that these Spanish sailors spent a fatal amount of time in the ocean and died of exposure.

At nearby Kittery, Maine, the average high temperatures for December and January are barely above freezing—34°F to 37°F (1°C to 3°C)—and the average low temperatures range from 14°F to 18°F (-8°C to -10° C). As the castaways stood and shivered, winds would have penetrated through their wet garments to the skin, setting their miserable frames shaking.

One of the body's first defenses against cold, shivering is an involuntary spasm of muscles to generate heat, beginning in the neck muscles, moving through the torso, and finally shimmering its way out to the extremities. If exposure becomes serious enough, shivering will stop, indicating a serious case of hypothermia.

Hypothermia, the condition that occurs when body temperature drops below what is required for normal metabolism and bodily functions, began to set in at least as soon as the first dripping-wet sailor landed on Boon Island. The human thermostat is a complex and not fully understood mechanism, with many cross linkages and neurochemical transmitters. Receptors found in the skin, stomach, and peripheral veins respond to changes in blood temperature and relay the information to the central

thermostat located in the hypothalamus just above the brain stem. Usually they tell the brain that everything is 98.6°F (37°C) or thereabouts.
When the core drops to 90°F (32°C), systems begin to fail. Core temperatures below this point are fatal if allowed to continue untreated.

Captain Deane and his crew were prime victims—standing soaked
through in conditions just above freezing without shelter or warm clothing as wind howled around them. As Deane explained it, "the weather
still continuing extream cold, with Snow and Rain." And the deadly conditions set to work, stealing whatever bit of heat it could from them. Wet
from their brief time in the surf and the falling precipitation, the men
were losing body warmth to the howling wind. At ten miles an hour,
wind more than doubles heat loss. Sitting down to seek relief from the
wind, they were transferring their heat to the rocks below them—and
being cooled further by snow and ice. They naturally radiated heat to
nearby objects, in this case rock, which in turn radiated the heat to the
sky—the majority of body heat lost in the cold is lost this way. The lower
the temperature difference between the surface of a person and nearby
objects, the less heat will be lost through radiation, which is why we rely
on clothes to keep us warm in cold weather.

The Boon Island castaways, however, were tragically bereft of any
warm garments—and any protection against radiant heat loss. Normally
each sailor went to sea with a coarse woolen coat, which insulates even
when wet, but all of the men abandoned ship without theirs, fearing the
weight and constraint in the rough and icy water more than the prospect
of freezing on shore. The men who fled the sinking *Nottingham Galley*
to Boon Island were likely clad only in linen shirts and trousers, or perhaps some cotton, none of which offered protection against the cold when
wet, or provided much warmth when dry. Some might have had woolen
britches or stockings, but these would have been of little comfort. Few
castaways in the history of shipwrecks were as thinly clad and unpro-
tected from exposure—in wet and subfreezing weather—as the victims
of the wreck of the *Nottingham Galley*. If in maritime history other shipwrecked sailors were more vulnerable than these, they didn't live to tell
about it.

After a prayer of thanksgiving—the crew were pious men—they set out to see what they could in the dark, according to Captain Deane, exploring the immediate vicinity of their landing area. They needed shelter from the still-raging storm, and for all they knew they might just stumble onto a settlement. They had been giving thanks to God for their salvation, but now it became apparent that the Almighty was still testing them. Much to their dismay the crew soon discovered that they were stranded on a very small island, as the captain put it, "without a Shovel full of Earth and destitute of the Growth of a single Shrub."

In the short time it took them to explore the isle—they could scramble from one side to the other in a minute or two—the ships' company found themselves trapped on a rock so jagged and serrated that they were reduced to crawling, "so very craggy that we coul'd not walk to keep our selves warm," as the captain recalled.

Boon Island is mostly comprised of metamorphic rock in small boulders—gray gneiss made primarily of quartz and feldspar—thrown up at awkward angles by the movement of the earth across the centuries. Layers of softer and harder rock, some more resistant to erosion than others, made the island's surface a mess of outcroppings, holes, and jagged edges that was virtually impossible to traverse. Here and there were flat spots where one could take a couple of steps, but that was about it.

Using their hands as well as their feet, the captain and his men clambered from the eastern end of Boon Island where the ship was breaking up, to the more sheltered leeward side. There they hunkered down on the cold rock while the nor'easter continued to blow. In this "disconsolate Condition they spent the first miserable Night."

Chapter 6

As dawn broke, the castaways got their first look at their island prison. It was an undisturbed expanse of jagged rock, rising to a hump in the middle. Nothing living could survive atop it—no vegetation of any kind offered cover from the winds. This they had noticed the previous night, but it was all the more evident as the unseen sun rose in the east behind a heavy shroud. Boon Island was ugly, gray, and cold. Unabatingly cold. And it was so small it took them no time to make the acquaintance of the entire thing. Frigid seas surrounded, beating rhythmically on the shore and reaching as far into the gloom as the men could see. Captain John Deane remembered it this way: "When the Day appeared, it presented us with a dismal Spectacle, a doleful little Spot in the Sea; of about an Hundred Yards square."

The weather was slow to clear; a thick overcast sky and a curtain of mist still enveloped them as the men took stock of their situation. The first order of business was to see what they could salvage from the wreck of the ship. Captain Deane was amazed when he returned to the site of their foundering. Some plank, canvas, and timber had washed up, and pieces of the masts, sails, and cordage floated out in the water, tangled and held in place by the ship's anchor, but that was about all that remained of the *Nottingham Galley*. The rest of the 120-ton vessel was completely gone, thoroughly vanished.

The crew were already in early stages of hypothermia, and it made the hours pass in a frigid haze. In their fragile condition, and with the somber, leaden, storm-wracked sky, the morning blended into the afternoon—and time blurred like the clouds and sea. The stranded sailors tried to keep track of the days and nights that followed, but they increasingly froze together into an undifferentiated mass. From day one they found it difficult to remember exactly what happened when.

Their survival instincts kindled in them, though a fire would not, no matter how hard they tried. They desperately wanted to raise their dwindling body temperatures, and just as important, they wanted a blaze to signal for help. And, of course, heat would be useful for cooking the meat they were sure they'd find, be it mussels, seals, fish, or birds. The men took to it resolutely, quite aware their lives depended upon it. The captain explained that they worked the flint, steel, and gunpowder that he salvaged, and then moved onto the ancient friction method—a "Drill of very swift Motion." Several crewmen worked at it for hours, kneeling on the cold rock, their hands fumbling with their tools. The ship's heavyset cook, Martin Downs, was particularly intent on raising a blaze, striking flint and steel over and over again, trying to shoot a spark into the gunpowder—spinning the drill and spinning the drill and spinning the drill in a futile attempt to create a life-giving spark.

Every effort failed. The island's suffocating dampness pervaded everything. They would continue trying to make a fire for more than a week before finally giving up.

The weather remained overcast into the second night. The men "stow'd one upon another, under the Canvas, in the best Manner they could Devise to keep each other warm." Their first glimmer of hope came when they awoke the following morning. The clouds began to clear, they could see off toward the horizon, and it brought a promising revelation—in the distance, where the sea met the sky, tantalizingly close, was the mainland. The piece of land closest to Boon Island, which the captain identified as Cape Neddick, extended out from the mainland a little over six miles distant from Boon Island. Deane tried to raise the spirits of his crew "with the Hopes of being discover'd by Fishing Shallops, or other Vessels occasionally passing that Way." Secretly, though, he realized that "rarely any Thing of this Kind happen'd at that unseasonable Time of the Year."

Though their morale was elevated slightly with the sight of the mainland, the castaways remained in a torpor of cold and hunger, and at least thirty-six hours passed on Boon Island before they accomplished anything useful. Members of the crew must have stood idly around whomever it was who futilely worked the flint and steel. Meanwhile, potentially useful materials, such as the spars, cordage, and sails tangled in the rocks and anchor, needed to be salvaged before being carried out to sea or destroyed.

Deane planned to use this wreckage, along with any tools they could find, for the construction of a shelter and an escape boat. If they could see the mainland, the men thought, they could reach it. But the retrieval of valuable resources sometimes meant wading into the icy surf with absolutely no means of warming later as temperatures hovered around the freezing point. The task was apparently too much for at least four members of the crew who were unresponsive and lethargic—"refusing to give Assistance even when required in necessary Matters," as the captain recalled.

Victims of hypothermia often experience inertia, becoming preoccupied with the sensation of cold; in severe cases they will simply lie down and die. Deane's lazy crewmen could have been suffering from hypothermia, but their behavior is also perfectly consistent with what disaster specialists call the Period of Recoil. The time immediately following an extremely stressful event is often characterized by "confusion" and "social fragmentation." During the first couple of days after a disaster, survivors often experience "denial and apathy," and they'll be surprised how physically exhausted they feel. From some combination of physiological and psychological suffering, some of the ship's company simply refused to follow orders and do the things necessary to promote their own survival.

Among those not working was Downs, the cook who had finally put down the flint and steel and now complained "he was almost starved." He didn't look well. In fact, the captain "ordered" him not to participate in the frigid salvage operation. Hypothermia strikes unevenly among groups of people, and in the case of the *Nottingham Galley*'s castaways, the ship's cook was its first victim. His craving for food was unusual for someone in his situation, since survivors typically experience very little hunger in the immediate aftermath of a disaster. If the cheese was at this time floating in the surf, the survivors were not yet desperate enough to eat it, for it had been "beaten into uncouth Forms by the violent Dashing of the Sea against the Rock."

Foolish. And by noon of the second day, Downs succumbed. "Our Cook, unused to the Hardships of a sea-faring Life," recalled the captain, "complain'd of violent Illness, which appear'd but too visibly in his Coutenance; he was lodg'd with two or three others, the most infirm, and died about Noon." Downs likely died of hypothermia-induced heart failure. Paleness and the dilation of pupils are among the first signs of hypothermia, which might have affected his countenance, and the violent pain, if it had been in his chest, could indicate heart trouble. When the body's core is chilled, the heart is forced to work harder to pump an increasingly viscous blood through a constricting circulatory system. To save itself the body limits blood flow to the extremities, where it becomes chilled, and collects it around the vital organs to keep them alive as long as possible. As the body makes these adjustments during the first three days of cold exposure, "there is a temporary continuous increase in venous pressure and this sudden surge of blood may cause overloading and failure of a vulnerable heart," notes Evan Lloyd, M.D., an authority on cold stress and hypothermia. The number of beats per minute falls and the heart's rhythm can become erratic, leading to fibrillation, which stops cardiac output completely.

Of all the positions on a trading vessel, the cook's was perhaps the must vulnerable in the case of a disaster like the one that had befallen the *Nottingham Galley*. He was the most likely to have been greenest at sea and, often to the disgust of a ship's crew, the most unskilled. Martin Downs was plausibly a member of the lowest rungs of English society, and it wouldn't have been surprising if he arrived on the *Nottingham Galley* malnourished or in ill health. Nearly anyone could get hired on as a ship's cook, especially in wartime when there were shortages of sailors. Landlubbers were often the first to die in a maritime crisis, while sailors were seasoned and callused by hard lives aboard ship. Occasional food or water deprivation among sailors helped condition them to situations of severe scarcity. A ship's cook was also exempt from most chores on deck, which meant Downs was likely not as physically fit as the other members of the crew. And most men with a few voyages to their name had been exposed to grueling and dangerous conditions and consequently developed a mental toughness that the cook seems to have lacked (if Deane's record of his whining and complaining were any indication).

The men deposited the corpse on the shoreline at low water and let the tide take it away. Several wondered if this was the best use of the cook's body—should they have eaten him to sustain themselves? Whether or not they said it aloud, it certainly went through their minds. "Several with my self afterwards aknowledged, had thot's of it," explained Deane.

The death of Downs only served to heighten the sense of danger the crew felt. Failure to produce a fire, and the constant threat of exposure, made the creation of some sort of shelter an urgent priority. According to Captain Deane, "the rest of our Men were generally so ill and bruised" two days after the wreck, "that but 4 or 5 of us were able to attempt anything for our safety." But they knew they had to do something to beat back the elements. They began to methodically scavenge the Boon Island coastline, finding "more Planks and Canvass sent us a shoar," and these they used to build a tent, "in a Triangular form." Each of the sides was about nine feet across. Apparently three spars were lashed together at the top, on which Deane reported that they flew a white flag in good weather as a beacon. The men all crawled inside, "where we housed ourselves from Wind and Weather."

The construction of the tent was the single most important thing the men of the *Nottingham Galley* could have done, saving them from the exposure that most certainly would have consumed them all, just as it had done to Martin Downs. Thirteen bodies lying side by side in the shelter kept the air temperature inside above freezing—barely so, but above freezing. Similar structures used in mountain rescue situations have the same effect.

Captain Deane took some satisfaction in the quality of the tent they built, but the placement of their new home proved to be dangerous. A cold and unwelcome surprise arrived in the night. "The sea Flowing high, came into our Tent, and carry'd away part of it," recalled Deane, "that we were necessitated to remove it to the highest Craggs of the Rock." The loss of materials in a slow rising tide seems wasteful and suggests a continuing lethargy among the ship's company.

Quite aside from its critical life-saving role, the tent gave the men something to focus on, and they continued to make improvements to it. The captain explained that he drew yarn from rope and with it "thatched the tent," which could "turn off 2 or 3 Hours of Rain, and skreen them, from the Asperities of the cold cutting Winds."

Huddled in their new tent, the men lay on the cold ground, and at some point, after a few days, a sailor became aware that he could no longer feel his feet. He tugged and pulled at his shoes, but it became clear that his feet had become so horribly swollen that he couldn't remove them. Several others began checking their own feet—only to discover that all were badly disfigured.

The men were suffering from either immersion foot or frostbite, or both. Otherwise known as trench foot, immersion foot strikes feet that are confined in wet and cold, though not necessarily freezing, conditions. Frostbite requires subfreezing temperatures. Both maladies have similar effects, with blood vessels failing to carry necessary oxygen and nutrients to cells, which begin to die. Symptoms include lack of feeling, swelling, and hardening of tissue; ulcers; and a red, blue, or purplish coloring that turns to gray or black with increasing severity. Deane noted that it was "extream cold" on the third day, so the problem may have been frostbite more than immersion foot. Either way, frostbite would certainly become a major problem.

The most menacing aspect of frostbite is the obstruction of blood supply to the tissues, often in conjunction with hypothermia—as the body draws blood into the core to consolidate heat and protect vital organs, blood vessels narrow to restrict flow, making the extremities more vulnerable to freezing. The most devastating harm is done when the cells lining the small capillaries and veins are damaged enough from the cold to allow the most liquid part of the blood—the serum—to leak out into the tissues, greatly diminishing blood flow. Blood cells can't remain suspended and so they clot, further restricting circulation. Without warmth and oxygen carried from the core tissues to the periphery, frostbitten extremities will die and turn to gangrene.

Deane and his men were keenly aware of—and very frightened by—this "mortification" of flesh. No one had wanted to take anything off in the cold, and walking on the jagged crags in bare feet was a particularly unpleasant proposition. But one of the sailors realized that he had better remove his shoes lest he lose all circulation in his feet.

The crewman took out a knife, which he'd held onto after abandoning ship, and began to carefully and painfully cut away at the shoe leather. Others watched and then found their own knives. Slicing through the leather—without also piercing the foot beneath—took quite some time, but finally the sailor was finished. And he found that what was inside his boot was even uglier than he thought—his stockings had fused to the skin. He started to peel, only to find to his horror that the skin was coming off with the sock. When he reached the end of his foot, gasping in pain, the toenails tore off, too. All the others discovered the same thing.

Screams filled the tent.

Revolted by the sight, the hideous smell, and the shrieks of the men as they unpeeled their stockings, the ship's boy alone among the castaways, could not bring himself to take off his shoes—or at least he didn't take them off soon enough. He would lose half of a foot because of it.

Chapter 7

THE HARBOR SEALS LOOKED DELICIOUS. TO THE HUNGRY CREW OF THE *Nottingham Galley,* the fat mammals were tempting, swimming just out of reach, like dinner afloat. If they could brain one of the beasts, they could eat for days. The meat would have to be consumed raw, but that would be a minor inconvenience. It was meat. Catching and killing a seal, though, would be a feat—the animals were both quick and smart—and the men were losing energy and ability fast. And there was all that water between them. The seals must not have liked the ravenous looks of their new English neighbors, for they soon departed never to be seen again.

Similarly elusive were birds. Gulls and cormorants and various ducks were frequently spotted—but they were also nearly impossible to trap or kill. Fish were another possibility, but no one among the castaways seems to have possessed the appropriate skills.

On a couple of occasions, however, the sea offered up to them a prize—a few bones of beef from the ship's stores. For English merchantmen, salted beef was a staple at sea, and properly cured it could last five years. Pummeled by the surf and eaten by the fish, the meat was even more unappealing than the cheese, but at least it was something to quell their cravings, and the men went for it hungrily. Hardly any flesh remained on the bones, but what was there was pounded into tiny bits and consumed. Starving men can't be picky.

When that was gone, it was back to the cheese. The pieces they could scavenge were divided into equal parts, and each portion was distributed by drawing lots. Each share amounted to about half a pound per man. Rationed, it might be stretched to feed a man for one week.

With their bellies tended to, at least for the time being, and their shelter erected, the stranded sailors turned their attention to building an escape boat out of the wreckage. Among the detritus left by the ship they salvaged a hammer, a calking mallet, and a cutlass. This last was cleverly converted into a saw by carving notches into its blade. They piled up assorted timbers and planking, pulled nails out of old sheathing, and collected oakum, sheet lead, long pieces of canvas, pump leather, and some new "Holland Duck," a high-quality sailcloth. It was just enough to do what they needed.

Working on the boat one day, someone spotted three sets of sail coming out of the Piscataqua at a distance of ten or so miles to the southwest. The sighting was shouted to the members of the crew laying in the tent, and in spite of extreme physical weakness, sore and shoeless feet, and bitter cold, each man crawled out and made his way over the hard crags and crevices to the southern tip of the island. Their spirits soared. As Captain John Deane explained, spying the ships "rejoyced us not a little." Deane and the men "believing our deliverance was now come," shouted and waved, screamed and shook pieces of sailcloth overhead.

But to no avail.

The ships were simply too far away to see men on the distant rock. Laying eyes on other boats—witnessing other human activity—was a lift to their collective morale, and the crew had some hope that ships on the move meant rescue was imminent. "We receiv'd no small encouragement from the sight of 'em," Deane recalled. "[It] gave us reason to conclude our distress might be known, by the wreck driving on shoar, and to presume were come out in search of us, and that they would daily do so when the weather would permit."

Still they believed the successful completion and voyage of the escape boat to the mainland was their best hope, and the only thing they could actively do to further their chances of survival. Time was not on their side, however; the ship's company became weaker and sicker by the day.

Only two others were sufficiently healthy to work on the boat with him, Deane recalled, and the weather did its best to discourage even them. It grew "so extream cold that we could seldom stay out of the Tent above

44

four hours in the day," he explained, "and some days do nothing at all." Normally the ship's carpenter would have taken the lead in any construction effort, but "thro' a violent Indisposition, [he] was utterly incapacitated from giving his necessary Assistance (and) almost his advice."

One of the men still able to work was a sailor the captain referred to as a "Swede." Scandinavian or no, he was built of something the others lacked. Frostbite had claimed both of his legs—his shin bones felt something like wooden boards attached to his knees—which meant that to help in the project he had to crawl across the rocky island, dragging his useless lower half behind him, back and forth from the work site to the tent. Others similarly beset lay in the tent and prayed.

Soon a majority of the ship's company were so debilitated from cold and hunger that they confined themselves to the tent twenty-four hours a day. Even those who ventured out to work did so only occasionally and otherwise stayed in the tent. The space inside was very tight for thirteen men, or twelve men and a presumably slighter ships' boy, and the odor in the tent, a byproduct of their rotting, frostbitten flesh, was increasingly noxious, especially for those who entered from the fresh air.

Every evening in the noxious confines of their shelter, Captain Deane would move among his men, and "daily dress'd their Ulcers," nursing them as best he could. He changed the dressings on their feet, legs, and hands, exposing their fetid, cold-induced sores; rock scrapes and cuts; and decaying digits. These they rinsed in seawater or urine. Hanging in the tent were two powder horns, into one of which the men relieved themselves and drew their own piss. In the traditional medicine of the day, urine was sometimes employed as a treatment for chilblains, small, itchy, and painful red areas that appear on the skin—especially on the feet and hands—in cold weather. These sores were the result of frozen, constricted blood vessels rewarming too quickly and flooding the adjacent tissue with blood. In serious cases the skin turns blue and becomes swollen, leaving cracks that infection can invade. Human urine is usually sterile, a mild disinfectant, and can be used to kill certain types of fungus. (Unbeknownst to the crew, however, they were shedding not only excess fluids when they relieved themselves, but they were also losing some of their precious core heat, as urination is yet another means of heat loss.)

After dousing themselves, they bound their wounds again "in Clean Rags, supplied from two Pieces of Linnen, amongst other Things, driven on Shore." And they "wrapp'd up their Legs in large swathing Bands of Oakum, pick'd and dried for that Purpose." One of the most useful materials salvaged from the wreck, oakum is a caulking substance composed of pine tar and horsehair or hemp fibers usually obtained from old rope. Packed between boards and joints to keep water out, it was used in the construction of homes and was an essential material in shipbuilding. The castaways found diverse uses for their limited supply of the stuff. Wrapped with the sailcloth, it served as insulation material for vulnerable frostbitten flesh, and it was also used for bedding to help protect the ship's company from the cold, hard rock.

The other powder horn in the tent contained drinking water, one of the few necessities the men had in abundance. "In regard to fresh water," noted Deane, they were "indifferently well supplied all of the Time by Rain, and melted Snow lodging in the concavities of the highest Part of the Rock," though the Captain went on to say that the highest tides could mix in sea spray with the drinking water, giving it a brackish taste. Occasionally drinking slightly salinated water, or even straight seawater, would have no serious medical effects.

When present snow was gathered and heaped just outside the tent within reach. Always critical, water became even more so due to the conditions. Anything less than a bountiful supply would have added to their list of problems. Dehydration compounds the threat from frostbite, and lying in one position, as most of them were doing, increases urine flow. Cold diuresis also causes the body to expel liquid—as blood retreats to the core, the kidneys conclude that the body is retaining too much fluid and increase urine output. This was all compounded by their hunger, because the early stages of starvation are characterized by intense thirst and frequent urination.

And they certainly had hunger. Their wracked bodies were doing everything possible to compensate. During periods of cold, water drains from circulating blood and is stored in the tissues. Blood viscosity can increase as much as 175 percent at low body temperatures, while total circulating blood volume can be down 25 percent after several days in the cold. Conversely, fasting thins the blood, so on Boon Island the cold and lack of food had countervailing tendencies. If hunger made the blood thinner than it would have otherwise been in the cold, it also increased the risk of tissue freezing.

While the captain and the Swede worked outside, the majority of the men lay in the tent sleeping or trying to sleep. The close quarters meant there was only enough room for each man to lie on his side pressed up against the man or men next to him. Lying so close, of course, had the advantage of conserving heat, but whenever someone fidgeted or thrashed about, which must have occurred a great deal on a rocky surface only lightly insulated by a thin layer of oakum, the disturbance woke everyone else. According to Deane this jostling was responsible for "occasioning some disputes." They must have each dreaded the end positions, which would have been the coldest. The black comedy inherent in the scene was rivaled by an equally humorous solution. It was decided that every two hours the captain would call out an order, presumably something like, "Shift!", at which time all of the men would awake to change sleeping positions.

As the men lay there, their bodies began to wear away wherever they touched the rock. Immobilized patients in hospitals are rotated regularly to prevent bed sores (also known as pressure sores). These open wounds occur where bones are close to the skin and pressed against an object for an extended period of time. If pressure sores can appear in relatively soft beds in a matter of days, their prevalence among the men of Boon Island, forced to lie on solid and irregular rock for weeks, can easily be imagined. The slight buffer of their oakum mattress provided little relief. Malnourishment only increased the problem of pressure sores, and as the bodies of the crew began to waste away, the wounds became excruciating. Their lower backs, hips, shoulder blades, heads, elbows, shoulders, heals, and ears all rubbed.

In the first stage of a pressure sore, the skin simply looks bruised. If the men were to have been rescued at that point, it would have taken about sixty days for these painful spots to heal. Come the second stage of the sore, and the skin breaks open, wearing away and forming an ulcer. Captain Deane recalled that it wasn't long before the ship's company on Boon Island became "ulcerous." In the third stage the sore worsens, forms a small crater, and extends beneath the surface of the skin into the tissue. As nerve damage occurs, pain increases, and at this point the risks of tissue death and infection are high. As the sore passes into its final phase, it delves into deeper tissue, including muscles and tendons, with potentially fatal complications. Still more serious are the infections they cause, which can become systemic and cause sepsis or blood poisoning. Captain Deane never mentioned the principal symptom of sepsis, which is the inflammation of the entire body. But without antibiotics members of the crew could have acquired sepsis while stranded and died later after the disease progressed.

With their painful sores, tight quarters, lack of privacy, hard rock, and the cold, sleep deprivation became an issue, which is why many of the men felt powerless and slept even during the day. During slumber, heat loss increases through the body's surface. The body produces 9 to 14 percent less heat during sleep, and people usually wake when they become cold to deal with the situation—someone too exhausted to rouse can slip into a fatal level of hypothermia. A lack of sleep would have combined with the cold to weaken the castaways' immune systems. Physical exhaustion, in turn, meant their bodies weren't generating heat. It was a downward spiral, with each problem encouraging the next

The captain described most of the ships' company as "so benumb'd and feeble as not able to stir." The best way to ward off hypothermia is through vigorous exercise, especially of the larger leg muscles. But that requires a greater than normal amount of calories—not an empty stomach. Starvation, like hypothermia, can cause severe lethargy, making the least exertion extremely exhausting, and a body needs food to generate heat. If those suffering on Boon Island had the strength to exercise, they would have spent 20 percent more energy in physical activity but would have gained 100 percent in terms of heat. Their fat stores weren't much help, either. Extra fat might keep a malnourished person warmer, but excess body fat is not readily converted into energy. What's more, extra body fat usually means a person is less fit, and the unfit are usually the first to perish, which was likely the case with Martin Downs, the ship's cook.

The enfeebling torpor brought on by starvation was compounded by hypothermia, which also immobilizes its victims. For most of those struggling to stay alive on Boon Island, the only choice was to use all of their limited energy to stay as warm as possible. This meant they had to lie together with their comrades, combining body heat, in the tent.

Despite all of these challenges, work continued on the boat. According to Deane a few members of the ship's company were able to emerge from the tent most days and put in a few hours' work on the primitive vessel. Just as their escape craft was nearing completion, the Carpenter's ax washed ashore, like a gift from the divine, making the remainder of the job that much easier. Deane stated that the ax was a present that "Providence so ordered." By December 20, nine days after their landing, they considered their work finished.

The vessel they built was a flat-bottomed craft three planks wide with two planks on each side and shortened boards across the bow and stern. Other pieces of wood were used as "stanchings" to cover gaps between the planks and to secure the sides to the bottom. Strips of sailcloth, pump leather, lead, and oakum were used to seal the seams. If there was any discussion about taking oakum from the bed on the floor of the tent, Deane didn't mention it. The fine Holland's Duck sailcloth was affixed around the perimeter of the boat to keep water out. According to Deane the boat also included a mast, a small sail, and paddles. For the time and place it was quite a feat, and the men were quite pleased with themselves.

December 21 was a fine day, with the ocean calmer than at any time since they had landed. The crude boat couldn't carry everyone; some would have to remain on the rock and await rescue. Captain Deane issued no orders; instead it seemed the entire crew discussed who should go, a bit of democracy that would have found no place at sea.

"I offering my self as one to adventure, which they agreed to, because I was the strongest, and therefore fittest to undergo the extremities we might be reduc'd to," Deane explained. "My Mate also offering himself, and desiring to accompany me, I was allow'd him with my brother, and four more." The Carpenter, though sick, was given a place in the boat, and he carried his hammer and ax with him.

Once they established who would pilot the craft—and who would crew—they had the larger task of launching. Simply hauling the boat to the shore was an arduous undertaking. The island's irregular rocks made walking difficult even without trying to move in tandem with a heavy boat, and it was all several of the men could do to leave the tent and stand upright, let alone grasp gunwales with frost-bitten hands. Not all of the men, perhaps only a handful, were well enough to help carry, but everyone roused himself from the tent to lend moral support. This was to be their deliverance. With a small boat, the mainland couldn't be that hard to reach.

The tide was running very high, so the seven men elected to go were obliged to wade deep into the frigid water to safely launch the craft. They pushed and pulled the boat out into water more than waste deep, and then they seemed to have had trouble climbing aboard in their weakened states. Only Captain Deane and one other managed to hoist themselves up and into the boat. Although a relatively calm day, there were still waves, or perhaps the surf had picked up since they began moving the vessel toward the sea.

Boon Island didn't want to let them go.

The captain and his crewmen rocked in the boat as the powerful Atlantic heaved underneath them. They knew they'd have to get past the line of breakers that pushed inevitably back toward the island. But their makeshift craft was unable to do so. As Deane recalled: "The swell of the Sea heav'd her along shore, and overset her upon us, (whereby we again narrowly escap'd drowning) and stav'd our poor boat all to pieces."

The hopes of the crew were dashed with the boat. Morale got worse when they realized that most if not all of the materials that went into their shipbuilding were lost, including the ax and hammer, which the

Carpenter had placed in the hull. As the men stood disconsolate, the breeze picked up, blowing cold on the water-soaked castaways. With the wind the seas offshore began to chop, as if taunting them.

Deane, in hindsight, was able to find some consolation, pointing out that "had we been at Sea in that imitation of a boat, in all probability must have perish'd, and the rest left behind had not better fare, because unable to help themselves."

But his spirits sank with the tools. The utter failure of the boat brought the survivors of the wreck to a new psychological low. Deane and his men were despairing:

We were now reduc'd to the most deplorable and mallancholy Circumstances imaginable, almost every Man but myself, weak to an extremity, and near starved with Hunger and Cold; their Hands and Feet frozen and mortified, with large and deep ulcers in their legs (the very smell offensive to those of us, who could creep into the air), and nothing to dress them with but a Piece of linen that was cast on shoar. No Fire, and the weather extream cold; our small stock of Cheese spent, and nothing to support our feeble Bodies but Rock-weed, and a few Muscles, scarce and difficult to get (at most not above two or three for each man a day). So that we had our miserable bodies perishing, and our poor disconsolate spirits overpowered, with the Deplorable prospect of starving, without any prospect of relief . . . the greater part of our company were ready die with horror and despair, without the least hopes of escaping.

Chapter 8

EVERY NIGHT THE MEN OF THE *NOTTINGHAM GALLEY* LOOKED FEARFULLY
to the sky—not to question Providence or search the clouds for weather
but to study the moon. The castaways had very quickly deduced the significance of the treeless and soilless nature of Boon Island—and it terrified
them. Clearly the small rock's complete lack of vegetation indicated that
the island was at times inundated with water, disappearing beneath the surface of the sea. Captain John Deane and his men were right to worry that
the ocean would rise to cover the island—waves have washed over Boon
before—but it would take a strong storm as well as a spring tide to do it.

The crew kept an anxious watch on the lunar phases and the rising
water, worrying about a so-called "spring tide," which appears after a full
or new moon. That's when the gravitational pull of both the moon and
the sun work together to cause extreme shifts in the tide. They noticed
the growing beds of rockweed as the low tide moved farther and farther
off the ledges that encircled the island, and they waited for the high tide
to climb the crags and flood their sad sanctuary, putting them out of their
misery. The ocean had already come creeping into their tent once before,
but at the time there were still higher places on the island to which to
retreat. Watching the mark of the tide rise every day was a sort of psychological water torture, compounding their already grievous problems of
cold and hunger.

But the full moon passed. They wouldn't drown in their beds—at least
not this month. The waning moon caused other problems, however—the
radically low tides were gone with it, leaving the seaweed and its precious
mussels underwater. It was becoming virtually impossible to find anything to eat. And the cheese was gone.

The pangs of hunger were unceasing. Captain Deane, he would later admit, considered eating one of his own fingers. He tasted his excrement to see if it could possibly be palatable. Anything to fill the maddening hole in his belly. This desire drove him back to the shore on a daily basis, searching for mussels. The captain was one of the few crew members who now left the tent. After the boat overturned, most of the other men seemed content to lie there and accept their fate.

As Deane recounted, he knew he couldn't simply sit still. Mussels weren't much—they had all the meat of a grasshopper on them—but they were something. When they could be found, each man got two or three of the little bivalves a day, cracking open the shell to peer inside. Deane learned that he couldn't palate mussels and chose to eat rockweed most of the time. Though he considered it easier to digest, the seaweed had its own downside. Deane felt that it led to constipation (though, in fact, seaweed is a laxative). Starvation itself usually causes constipation until the body's immune system breaks down, reducing the ability to resist bacterial infection, at which time diarrhea results.

The captain plunged his hands again and again into the icy waves to fish out what food he could find in the rocks. "I have gone myself (no other Person being able) several days at low water," he recalled, "and could get no more than two or three at Piece, and have frequently been in danger of losing my hands and arms by putting them so often in the water."

It got so bad with the rising waters that, finding little rockweed, Deane brought a piece of "green hide being thrown up by the sea (fasten'd to a piece of the Main-Yard)" back to the tent, where it was "minc'd" to bits and swallowed. This would have been a piece of salt beef from the *Nottingham Galley*'s stores that floated in the ocean for between two and three weeks.

Christmas Day came, though losing track of time, they argued which day that actually was, and brought with it a gift of sorts. A seagull landed nearby. And it sat there long enough—and close enough—that the first mate was able to brain it with a saucepan, giving the men yet more meat. They had to eat the bird raw, and it was on the small side, "scarce every one a mouthful," Captain Deane noted, but it was something to placate their greedy stomachs. And, again, it was meat.

Without the diligence of their captain, as he explained later, the men would have simply starved and been frozen to death on the rock. He did everything he could for his crew. But such was the obligation of the commander of a vessel, especially one who was healthier than the men in his charge.

Healthier indeed. Deane, as he noted again and again, was in the best condition of all of the ship's company. Why might this have been? He probably didn't get to eat more than his share of their stores. Given the circumstances, it's doubtful the other castaways would have allowed it. Deane argued that he kept his health because he kept himself moving, expending more energy than the rest in searching for food. For his extra work Deane "reap'd one Benefit, for maintaining of Warmth by Action, preserv'd a due Circulation of Blood, imparting a benign Influence to the whole System."

When it comes to survival in cold conditions, all men are not created equal. A slow metabolism might have helped the captain, and he might have begun the journey with more fat on his body, but not so much that he was unfit. Perhaps he had just enough fat to keep him warm as an insulator and be a source of latent heat energy. The rate of survival in cold weather situations can be directly related to body mass. Since heat is lost through the skin, smaller people, particularly children, are more vulnerable to heat loss because the total surface area of their skin is a higher ratio to body volume. Conversely, stocky people are better at retaining heat.

Some people have simply evolved to survive better in the cold. Because the origin of the species was in hot climates, the body is much more adaptable to high temperatures than low ones. But people with ancestors who lived in colder climates are better able to survive cold stress than their fair-weather cousins. Africans are three to six times more susceptible to frostbite than Europeans and do not increase their heat production as efficiently. Peoples from cold climates, like Eskimos, Lapps, and Nordics, have developed heightened mechanisms that make them more resistant to frostbite.

No matter where it resides, the human body has evolved to defend itself from the cold. It doesn't give up on its frozen extremities without a fight. A process called vasodilation, or the "hunting reaction," takes place, during which the blood vessels dilate every seven to ten minutes, providing warm blood to threatened tissues, especially in the fingers and toes. In time, if the body's core becomes too cold, vasodilation will stop as the body decides to prioritize the protection of vital organs. This blood flow regulator is stronger in people whose genes come from cold climes than in people who have evolved in other regions. Acclimation, as well as evolution, may also build resistance to frostbite.

Various other chemical and physiological differences can enhance functioning and survival in cold weather, too. For example, among people of a European background, those with type A or B blood are less likely to get frostbite than those with type O. Captain Deane likely benefited from a combination of body mass, metabolism, ethnicity, and/or blood type.

Rank and social position gave the captain yet another advantage. He slept with the ship's boy right on top of him as a human blanket. Maybe he thought he was helping the boy by protecting him from the cold rocks, maybe he wanted to maximize body heat. Whatever the reason, Deane must have spent some hours on his back as well, in uncomfortably intimate contact with the unnamed lad.

As the weeks passed, Captain Deane watched the bodies of his men break down. Exposure to the cold and starvation were conspiring to impose their miseries. Studies have shown that the average man has 141,000 calories stored in fat tissue, 24,000 in muscle mass, and 300 in glycogen. Theoretically that's enough calories to last eighty days or more. What the body lacks, though, is the glucose required by the brain, eyes, and gonads. After thirty-six hours of fasting, protein is burned, converting amino acids into glucose, and people typically begin to experience headaches, dry eyes, and edginess. After seventy-two hours without food, they become tired, weepy, and develop a bad taste in their mouths.

Most people can live for about sixty days without food. But among the bereft crew of the *Nottingham Galley,* it was not just the lack of food that beset them, but the way starvation coupled with cold to compound their problems. In studies, semistarving people have complained of feeling cold in the middle of summer, shivering under three or four blankets during the hottest days of July, body temperatures falling as much as five degrees. Similarly, other research has shown a calorie-deprived man wearing two suits and two topcoats in the middle of summer and still unable to keep warm.

And there were Deane and his fellow castaways, dressed in tatters, huddled beneath a thin sail canvas, with wet oakum instead of blankets, in the frozen temperatures of December.

The captain wasn't the only crew member who refused to give up. While his companions wallowed in their own misery, the "Swede" retained some hope and enterprise. From the beginning the sailor the captain called "a stout, brave Fellow" had preferred a simpler and smaller raft to a full-fledged boat as a way off the island—and despite the sinking of their last vessel, he still thought going for help would be the company's salvation. He'd already decided that no one was coming for them.

The escape boat now a bitter memory, the Swede began to put his ideas into practice. Over the course of the next week, he labored under staggeringly difficult conditions, crawling on his hands and knees, pulling and dragging the necessary materials together. While he was working, the Swede's hands suffered under a constant threat of frostbite. The construction of the raft, as the captain described it, would have to be accomplished "without Tools, and, almost without Hands." Indeed anyone familiar with subfreezing weather knows how difficult it can be to manipulate tools and materials with precision when his hands get cold. Studies have shown that when hand surface temperature reaches 55°F (12.8°C), manual performance begins to become impaired. Take the temperature down several more degrees, and dexterity degrades even further.

Nevertheless, the Swede gathered his resources around him on the rock and then cleared the foreyard—the lowest part of the foremast— from a tangle of "junk, sailcloth, and lumber." After that he managed to split the twelve-foot foreyard down the middle and joined the two pieces together by thin four-foot-long planks, "first Spiking, then seizing them firm." Two hammocks on deck were rigged for sails, and three paddles were procured, two to propel the craft and the third to serve as a spare.

As the raft neared completion, the Swede tried to persuade the captain to come along on the escape attempt. Deane wanted none of it. He thought a trip on the Swede's primitive boat was an act of suicide. The captain "deliberately weighing the difficulties of the Adventure, judg'd them, rationally speaking, unsurmountable, that Persons already so much reduc'd, must, in so severe a Season, set up to the Waist in Water, 10 or 12 hours at least, with the utmost favor of the Wind, Tide, and Weather."

Escape rafts are always high-risk vessels. Because of the very nature of their construction—usually accomplished with few tools and whatever materials might be on hand—they often take on a great deal of water. That was the case in the wreck of the *Medusa* off the coast of Africa in 1816, a terrible tale with much in common with the *Nottingham Galley*, but at least the four hundred passengers and crew members stranded by that ship found themselves in warm equatorial latitudes.

Captain Deane declined the Swede's invitation, but the disabled castaway was not dissuaded, asking a third man who also possessed notably superior health. The new vessel was finally deemed ready on December 26 or 27, two weeks after the men landed on Boon Island. Just the day before another sail had been seen coming out of the Piscataqua, but it too had disappeared without coming anywhere near their damned isle. Like the Swede, most of the men had decided by this time that no one was coming for them. Desperate measures were required, so they gathered their collective strength, hauled the raft down to the edge of the sea, and set about trying to help the Swede as best they could.

One among them, though, made an impassioned plea against the journey. According to Deane, the first mate was vehement and unequivocal—he "strenuously oppos'd it, on account 'twas so late (being 2 in the afternoon)." The Swede had decided the time was right—the wind was pushing toward the mainland. The big man with the foreign accent—whether courageous or foolish—persisted in making the case to launch the raft immediately, noting that there would be a full moon that night. For all the concerns Deane himself had, he overruled the first mate. Determined as the Swede was, he probably would have shoved off whatever the officers decided.

The shipwrecked company, frantic for any sign of hope, made the Swede and his companion agree to have a fire built on shore as a signal that they had made it safely to the mainland. "Committing the enterprise to God's Blessing," the Swede was placed on the raft, since he couldn't wade into the water on his incapacitated legs. The other sailor climbed aboard on his own, and Captain Deane pushed them off toward the mainland six miles distant. They paddled out a little way—and the story became tragically familiar.

"The Swell, rowling very high, soon overset them as it did our boat," the captain recalled. The makeshift mast and sail on the little raft were lost. A strong swimmer, the Swede returned to shore with no difficulty. But, Deane explained, the other man struggled, "being no swimmer," so the captain dove in and dragged the drowning sailor back to the rock. Nearly dead from the sea, the man had had enough. Not so the Swede.

Standing beside the Swede, both men dripping wet, Captain Deane urged his crewman not to make another attempt. According to Deane, the Swede, on his knees, simultaneously pathetic and heroic, begged the captain to join him on the raft, while insisting that he would make another try all by himself if necessary.

What point was there sitting on a rock and waiting to die?

To most of the crew, climbing aboard the raft looked hopeless and deadly. Nevertheless, another sailor came forward to throw his lot in with the Swede's, an act that showed either great courage, or more likely, an act of utter desperation. The men knew they couldn't survive much longer.

The Swede and the new volunteer would make another attempt, and perhaps understanding that they needed a miracle, the stout man asked everyone to promise to pray for their safe deliverance to the mainland. The two men were set on the raft and soon were paddling slowly away from Boon Island. Instead of returning to the shelter of the tent, all of the remaining survivors gathered on a ledge facing west to watch the raft as it inched its way across the wide stretch of sea that separated the castaways from food and beds. The sickly survivors remained on the ledge for the rest of the afternoon, honoring the Swede's request of prayer. The sun sank before their eyes, setting behind the band of evergreen on the mainland, and with the dying light of day, they could see that the raft was halfway across. One by one the castaways returned to the tent.

That night, lying huddled together on their sore, frozen, emaciated bodies—no doubt thinking about their comrades paddling across the silver, moonlit sea—the men listened as the wind drummed ominously on the sailcloth of their tent.

The captain and crew had come to the stark realization that they were not going to be accidentally discovered. Starving people are known to experience long bouts of depression interrupted by brief periods of elation—the men had known plenty of the former and were beginning to feel the latter. Their two saviors had been on their way as darkness fell. But the tent luffed ominously in the winds. Were they heavy enough to overturn the raft or keep it from reaching shore? Would the resulting waves capsize their friends?

The sight of the raft halfway across the channel between Boon and the mainland raised their hopes, and the crew passed a few days in better spirits. And then one afternoon, two days after the raft had launched, morale soared.

Standing outside the tent, one of the castaways began to holler. He'd been staring longingly at the mainland, as the men often did, and suddenly spied above the trees a wisp of rising smoke from the hill where the Swede and his raft mate had promised to set a fire if they succeeded in making landfall. Could it be their salvation? Was this the promised sign?

The men struggled out of the tent and stood on the cold crags, staring across the sea, arms around one another, the sturdier sailors helping to keep their weakened comrades upright so they could see for themselves. It was unmistakable—wafting up over the spruces was a column of smoke. A fire was burning on the shore, and a wave of joy washed over the castaways. As Captain Deane put it, the sign of smoke was "interpreted by them as a Token of speedy Deliverance. This Flush of Hope, Under God, subserv'd for a Time to support them."

Their good cheer was short-lived, however. A day passed with no sign of rescuers. Then another. And another. The men assumed their rescuers were having difficulty procuring a vessel. With every day that a boat did not arrive, their spirits sank like a stone into the sea. They tried to reason that the freezing over of rivers might have delayed the launch of a rescue, but as the days passed, so did any hope they might have had, and the black cloud of inevitability returned.

Chapter 9

ON BOON ISLAND EVERY BIT OF GOOD NEWS, EVERY OCCASION TO HOPE, was quickly followed by a return to despair. For the ship's carpenter, who had been sick almost since the night of the wreck, it came not long after they ate the seagull. Forty-seven years old, "a fat Man, and naturally of a dull, heavy, Phlegmatick Constitution and Disposition," according to Captain John Deane, the Carpenter had lost the use of his feet in the early days, much like the Swede. He had rallied himself on occasions to try and help supervise the construction of the boat, but he usually found he was too weak to contribute much to the effort. Even so, he had insisted on taking a place on the failed first craft, which left him wet and caked in icy clothes. Since then he'd complained of back pain and stiffness in his neck, which grew so bad he couldn't move his head.

He was in even worse shape than he knew. His lungs had begun to fill with phlegm, which he was unable to discharge. This was likely the result of edema, which is not uncommon in cases of both hypothermia and starvation and occurs even in normal temperatures when a person lies in the same position for days at a time. The fluid could have become infected, causing pneumonia, or it might have put an additional strain on the heart leading to heart failure. He might have had a small heart attack, which would explain the back and neck stiffness, though this could also be due to his immobilization on the rock

Captain Deane said that they prayed over the Carpenter and did what they could to help him, but he became incommunicable, "sensible tho' speechless." And his condition worsened quickly. Each night toward the end of December, the twelve castaways would lie crowded together in the tent, listening for the raspy breathing of the Carpenter. Laboring to breathe, he'd keep some of them awake into the wee hours. And then, according to Deane, one evening at about midnight the captain "enquired of them that lay next to him, who told me, he was dead." The night passed with the corpse practically on top of several crew members, who couldn't be bothered to move it. As Deane put it, they "suffered the Body to remain with us 'till morning."

Obviously the need for nourishment was becoming extreme, but the psychology of hunger was also taking a toll. Studies show that after a few days, food deprivation moves from a distraction to an obsession. Lack of food causes "apathy, depression, emotional instability, and impairment of concentration and memory." Victims of starvation can begin to lose their humanity and behave as "wild beasts."

When the sun came up, Captain Deane exited the tent on his now regular search for mussels, rockweed, or anything else potentially edible. On his way out he made it known that he "desir'd them who were best able to remove it [the body]." He returned to the tent before noon that day with very little or no food. To his annoyance the corpse was still there in the crowded tent. He was exasperated, having been out working while the rest of the men couldn't even muster enough strength or determina-tion to drag a dead body just a few feet out of their midst. The captain asked why they hadn't removed the Carpenter, to which the others replied that they were unable.

Angered, Deane took action himself, as he reported, tying a rope to the Carpenter's still fat torso. Someone must have offered to help him, because he explained that "with some difficulty we got it out of the tent." Heaving on the rope with the Carpenter on the other end, was a challenge even for the relatively healthy Deane, and he felt woozy. But the body was at least outside now. It could be brought down to the shore and disposed of later. Deane needed to lie down, and the captain crawled into the tent again. No sooner did he do so than the men asked him the question.

From the beginning, cannibalism has been one of the great taboos of Western civilization. With themselves at the center of the world, the ancient Greeks placed less-civilized peoples on concentric circles extending outward to a periphery where cannibals lurked with other hideous hybrids of man and beast. The villains of Greek mythology were frequently cannibalistic. The barbarian invaders of early medieval Europe, especially the Tartars, were characterized as "houndish cannibals," and Mongols, Turks, and Muslims, too, were similarly accused of man eating.

The residents of Christendom saw themselves above such a thing, even though the Christian sacrament of Holy Communion exists in a peculiar juxtaposition to cannibalism. Roman Catholic doctrine holds that wine and bread miraculously become transformed into the actual blood and body of Christ through the process of transubstantiation. The sacrament of Communion itself represents a sort of representational cannibalism, however the sacrament's symbolic and holy nature made actual human cannibalism seem an especially great evil. If Holy Communion with God changed man into Christ, then perhaps eating another human being changed man into beast.

During the Crusades, word arrived back in Europe that starving Crusaders had been forced to consume Saracens. The news made Christians question the ethics of the whole crusading enterprise, though Richard the Lionheart had an answer to the critics—he explained that Muslims were not really human. Eating the enemy not only terrorized him, but also dehumanized him. And beasts were always fair game.

Like the ancient Greeks before them, Medieval and Renaissance Europeans found actual cannibals as they pressed outward to explore the world. Marco Polo discovered man-eaters on his travels to the East. The existence of cannibalism in other cultures encountered by Spanish and French explorers, such as the Aztecs or the Caribs, the people from whom the Caribbean got its name, was used to justify conquest and enslavement by Europeans. The shockingly large scale on which the Aztecs were known to practice human sacrifice and cannibalism encouraged a feeling of moral superiority among their brutal Spanish conquerors.

Around the time the men of the *Nottingham Galley* were suffering on their rock, travel and shipwreck narratives both real and imagined were ragingly popular among Europe's reading public, and many of these featured cannibalism. In a most famous example, Daniel Defoe's marooned

Robinson Crusoe is constantly fearful of being cannibalized by local savages on nearby islands, and reforming the savage named "Friday" of his man-eating habit is at the top of Robinson's agenda.

As they obsessed over the flesh eating practiced by far-flung peoples they considered barbarians, Europeans were forced to draw a sharp distinction between ceremonial and cultural cannibalism on the one hand, and survival cannibalism on the other. Their travels were taking them off to the far corners of the world, and they occasionally found themselves in desperate straits that required them to eat each other. As their ships smashed in storms, starving castaways in lifeboats were reduced to the most base of acts simply to survive.

European Christians needed an intellectual framework to justify their own instances of cannibalism, but that was problematic. Was all cannibalism an unnatural abomination, as it was conventionally understood, or was it justified under certain circumstances? If barbaric peoples ate each other, could civilized men ever do likewise and remain civilized? Yes, they could, so long as the victim's death was natural and it was a survival situation. That was what the law came to hold. Furthermore, if someone had to die and be eaten so that others might live, killing became legal as long as it was done by drawing lots, a tradition that goes back to the Hebrew Testament story of Jonah. But from a cultural and visceral point of view, the notion that man eating is an unnatural and repulsive act under any circumstance persisted in Western society.

The men of the *Nottingham Galley* were forced to consider something that a long line of sailors before and after wrestled with. In 1765 the American merchant ship *Peggy* was crippled and left adrift in a terrible Atlantic storm, and when food became exhausted, the only slave on the ship was killed and eaten. In 1816, the French frigate-turned-cargo-ship *Medusa* ran aground on its way to Senegal. The 150 castaways on an ill-conceived escape raft were driven to madness, murdering each other in a series of pitched battles—and feeding off the dead. In 1821 the whaling vessel *Essex* was rammed and sunk by a whale, inspiring Herman Melville's *Moby Dick*. As sailors died on the lifeboats, their bodies were eaten by their comrades. The wreck of the English yacht *Mignonette* led to the cannibalizing of the dying ship's boy by the captain and one of the crew. Rescued a short while later, they confessed and were found guilty of murder, but a reprieve from the Crown greatly reduced their sentence.

The idea of eating the Carpenter was, as Captain Deane claimed, "most grievous and shocking," and it prompted a lengthy debate about "lawfullness and sinfulness on the one Hand; and absolute Necessity on the other." Several men, including First Mate Christopher Langman, Boatswain George Mellen, and two others, wanted no part of it, calling "(eating the Carpenter) a heinous Sin." Those who argued for cannibalism out of necessity pointed to their deteriorating physical conditions. Two men had by this time died on the island, at least in part from starvation, and two others were lost on the raft, and the rest, it was argued, were at their "last Exreamity."

In the end the captain reports that he decided that "Judgment, Conscience, &c. were oblig'd to submit to the more prevailing arguments of our craving appetites." After "maturely weighing all Circumstances, pronounc'd in Favor of the Majority, arguing the improbability of it being a Sin to eat Humane Flesh in case of such necessity, provided they were no ways accessary to the taking away of Life."

It was one thing to decide to commit the act of cannibalism. It was another altogether to play the role of butcher, a job nobody wanted. Everyone in the tent understood that Captain Deane was the most logical choice for this repellent task. He had the most physical strength remaining and the best hands, and he had been apprenticed to a butcher. He knew how to cut meat from bone. But did he have the character to do such a thing? He would have to.

Sometime during the course of the afternoon Deane reemerged from the tent to return to the corpse of the Carpenter. He wasn't alone but didn't say who was with him. They resolved to cut the most distinctly human parts from the rest of the corpse, including the skin, hands, feet, and head, which the captain said, were deposited into the ocean. The horrible task took hours. By sunset they were finished.

"I then cut part of the flesh in thin Slices, and washing it in the saltwater, brought it to the Tent, and oblig'd the men to eat Rockweed along with it, to serve instead of bread." That night most of them ate the grue-some meal but those who had argued against it stood their ground and refused. By morning, however, these dissenters had changed their minds, and, as Deane noted, "earnestly desir'd to partake with the rest."

After they all ate the Carpenter, Deane noticed that the behavior of the men changed:

> *I found (in a few days) their very natural dispositions chang'd, and that affectionate, peaceable temper they had all along hitherto discover'd totally lost; their eyes staring and looking wild, their Coun-tenances fierce and barbarous, and instead of obeying my Commands (as they had universally and readily done before) I found all I cou'd say (even prayers and entreaties vain and fruitless) nothing now being to be heard but brutish quarrels, with horrid Oaths and Imprecations, instead of that quiet submissive spirit of Prayer and supplication we had before enjoy'd.*

The meat satisfied the cravings of the crew, and according to Deane they hungered for more. The captain did his best to guard and ration the meat, but he worried what would happen once it was gone. Immediate rescue would be necessary, lest "we be forc'd to feed upon the living: which we must certainly have done, had we staid a few days longer." It's not dif-ficult to guess what would happen next—the weakest among them would have no place to run and no place to hide on their small rocky prison.

Studies have shown that barbarism seems to naturally follow can-nibalism in a process that plays out exactly as Deane reported. One case of a deliberately food-deprived group showed that in some ways they did become less human. The test subjects disliked being touched or caressed, and emotional responses like fear, love, and shame became dulled. Researchers in another case remarked on starvation's dehuman-izing effects, finding that extreme hunger "reduced people to the level of animals." One group of women were said to have behaved as "wild beasts."

Not only did the ingestion of human flesh damage the minds (and morals) of his men, but Deane believed it decayed their bodies as well.

He said it had "an ill Effect about their Ulcers and Sores, endangering a Mortification more than ever." To the captain, with all his talk of the Lord, it must have made sense that the corruption of their souls would be followed by the decay of their physical bodies, just as it might be hoped that the eating of the Host in Holy Communion might lead to healing.

On the morning of January 2, Captain Deane emerged from the tent as he had every morning since the wreck to search for food and perhaps to relieve himself. The winter wind briskly beat against the canvas as he rose to his feet. Looking toward the mainland, he saw it: Stover's shallop under full sail about halfway across, making for Boon Island. He immediately cried out hoarsely, "A sail! A sail!" Rendered speechless by the joy of the moment, Deane could find no other words. From the tent everyone, no matter how weak and infirm, "instantly thrust out his Head to see so desirable Sight and to express the Raptures diffus'd throughout the whole Company, upon the Prospect of so sudden and unexpected a Deliverance . . .'twas Life from the Dead."

Wary of coming closer to the treacherous ledges, the shallop anchored about a hundred yards off the southwest corner of the rock. The wait until noon for smoother water was maddening for Deane and the other survivors. "Expectations of Deliverance, and fears of miscarriage, hurry'd our weak and disorder'd spirits strangely." With the rising tide the shallop moved in closer so that the captain could shout back and forth to the men in the boat, "giving them account of our miseries."

The captain was careful about what he said, though. He recalled later that he didn't tell them that they were starving because he wished first for an immediate evacuation and second for them to come ashore and provide fire. He didn't want his would-be rescuers to sail away immediately for provisions. Though they were all starving—with only the remainders of the human carcass left to eat—the captain apparently wanted to manage the situation in such a way that deprioritized food. He, too, might well have wanted to avoid the subject because he feared the reaction of the rescuers to the fate of the Carpenter. For men in such desperate straits it was a peculiar calculation.

Finally, after much effort, one of the men from the shallop came ashore in a small canoe. Deane could see from the man's face that his physical appearance rendered the man speechless. The shock was magnified upon viewing the rest of the survivors in the tent. "Our flesh so wasted, and our looks so ghastly and frightful, that it was really a very dismal prospect." After building the fire and unsuccessfully trying to evacuate Deane, the men in the shallop, who had brought so much hope with their arrival, sailed off amid the thickening clouds.

"'Twas a very uncomfortable sight," Deane remembered, "to see our worthy friends in the Shallop stand away from shore without us." But in hindsight Deane recognized that they were all fortunate not to have been aboard the small boat in the coming storm, for "had we been with them, we must have perish'd, not having sufficient strength to help ourselves."

Meanwhile, as Stover's sailboat got underway, the castaways continued to build their fire in the middle of the tent, but foolishly neglected to vent it, nearly smoking themselves out. When a hole had been cut and the smoke had cleared, they waited out the storm to the sound of their meat sizzling on the fire. Apparently they liked the smell—according to the captain the men wanted more than their allotted portions. Since rescue was imminent, some argued for larger shares of the Carpenter's flesh. The captain said he gave them a second helping, but still it was not enough.

"The next day our Men urging me vehemently for more flesh, I gave them a little more than usual, but not to their satisfaction, for they wou'd certainly have eat up the whole at once."

It became hard to justify rationing the meat further, since there was so little left and deliverance seemed imminent. They just had to wait out the weather, which couldn't last.

Perhaps, too, they were not certain that they wanted human meat lying around when the rescuers came back.

Part III

The Tale of a Rebellious Crew

Chapter 10

THE NIGHT BEFORE THE SLOOPS ARRIVED TO RESCUE THEM, FIRST MATE Christopher Langman had a dream. Gripped by fever, fitful on his bed of hard rocks, he saw the sails of a ship rise up above the waves to carry the men of the *Nottingham Galley* away. The next day the gunner had the same vision—only he was waking and it was real. Langman had told him to leave the tent and look for a boat, because he had a feeling it was coming. And it was. January 4, twenty-four days after their ship was scuttled, the crew were finally delivered.

Four sloops arrived at the island, graceful, midsize sailboats that couldn't have been any more welcome, and canoes were dispatched to fetch the castaways. Many of the survivors were able to board of their own power, but others were carried. As Langman recalled: "several of us had our Legs so frozen, and were so weak that we could not walk."

Once aboard, the men were given a small bit of nourishment, according to Langman. "These Gentlemen took great care of us, and would not suffer us to eat or drink but a little at a time, lest it should do us hurt." The wind did the rest, whisking the fleet past the Isles of Shoals to the mouth of the Piscataqua River as the sun receded into the forests on the shore. Captain John Deane and Miles Whitworth were ferried off to Captain Jethro Furber's house, while the rest of the wretches were taken to Portsmouth.

"Night we arrived at Piscataqua in New England," Langman remembered, "where we were all provided for." The castaways were transported from the docks to a tavern with rooms, where they would begin their long convalescence.

At the tavern, the crew "[had] a Doctor appointed to look after us," Langman noted gratefully. And the services of Doctor Packer were very much in demand. The physician had grim work ahead, amassing a small pile of amputated fingers and toes. The ship's boy, who had decided not to remove his shoes on the island, lost half of one foot. Despite all of the pain and loss, the men were overjoyed to be back in society with its hot food and warm beds.

Jasper Deane joined his brother and Whitworth—the gentlemen passengers of the *Nottingham Galley*—in private homes while the men recuperated in the public house provided for them. Several days into their recovery, Captain Deane came to the inn to see his men, and the mood of the crew quickly changed. Deane hadn't come calling out of compassion, at least as Langman saw it.

Deane brought with him his protest, a document that he said contained the truth of their shipwreck and the circumstances behind it, and he wanted the signatures of the ranking members of the ship's company— the first mate and the boatswain. He easily acquired the first, stopping by Langman's side and imploring the mate—who was still "very ill of a Flux and Fever"—to put his name down. Langman put quill to paper.

Then something curious happened. George White, who had never before been referred to as boatswain, and who was also very unwell, signed as the boatswain. In all the documentation on the voyage, Nicholas Mellen had been the only crew member with the title of boatswain. White is described as "only a "sailor," and he even swore to this under oath.

Ships and islands are close places and make close friends or bitter enemies. The actual boatswain, Nicholas Mellen, had developed a fierce hatred of John Deane. He had had numerous run-ins with the captain, both during the crossing and on the island, and would never help him if he could avoid doing so. After he said his peace, the captain turned and simply dubbed White the new boatswain on the spot. White had been among the healthiest of the men on Boon, but his plunge into the Atlantic—when he and the Swede capsized on the Swede's first raft—seemed to have taken its toll. In the tavern, he sat in bed feeling as sickly as the rest of them and signed without much drama. But it wasn't because he wanted to help the captain. He was afraid of what Deane might do if he refused. White explained later that he signed the protest "for fear of being put of out his Lodgings by the Captain, while he was both sick and lame."

Having gotten what he wanted, Deane excused himself and left the men, who stayed at the inn for another few weeks while their captain made the social rounds in Portsmouth, telling his story to all who would listen. According to the locals who visited the convalescing crew, Deane had made quite an impression on the town's residents ever since he first came ashore and burst into Captain Furber's home. He terrified the Furber family on that night, and according to Langman, he scared the Furber children further during his stay, telling them "he would have made a Frigasy out of them, if he had had 'em in Boon Island." With tales like this, the first mate said, Captain Deane "frighten'd the People that heard him; and made them esteem him as a Brute, as he was."

The citizens of Portsmouth began to wonder if Deane was really the hero he said he was in his story, and the compassion and curiosity they had for the captain began to recede like the tide. Captain Furber was reportedly disgusted with Deane's antics. "Instead of being thankful to God for his own and our Deliverance, he returned with the Dog to his Vomit, and behav'd himself so brutishly, that his Friend Captain Furber was obliged to turn him out of his House," remembered Langman, Mellen, and White.

Langman, Mellen, and White felt betrayed. And Langman and White became dismayed they'd corroborated Deane's account. From the outset of the journey to the consumption of the Carpenter, what they remembered and what Deane had described were very different events. The captain, they said, "compell'd us to sign what our Illness made us uncapable to understand."

So they sought out Judge Samuel Penhallow, magistrate of Portsmouth—the same judge to whom Deane had told his story, the same judge who had passed the tale on to Cotton Mather—to tell him the real truth of the *Nottingham Galley*'s ordeal.

Samuel Penhallow had a hand in almost every aspect of New Hampshire's business and civic life. Justice of the peace, governor's councillor, writer of history—he was, like all good Calvinists, a busy man. At various times the judge would hold a host of the colony's most prestigious offices, and his influence spread throughout New England.

Born in Cornwall County, England, Penhallow was offered the opportunity to travel to New England as a missionary, and was promised twenty pounds of sterling a year for three years, by the Society for Propagating the Gospel Among Indians in America. He arrived in the colonies in Charleston, South Carolina, but before long he'd moved north to Portsmouth. There he met the daughter of John Cutt, one of Portsmouth's most powerful and richest merchants. Marrying into the Cutt family, Penhallow inherited extensive business interests and property, including most of the town itself. He won greater wealth in trade and was made a magistrate, helping extend the Queen's laws into this remote corner of her empire.

Perhaps foremost on the judge's mind in January 1711 were the delay in the sailing of the mast fleet and the war with the Indians, which he watched with a keen curiosity. Furiously scratching down notes for what would become his *History of the War of New England with the Eastern Indians, or a Narrative of Their Continued Perfidy and Cruelty,* Penhallow was still studying the participation of local tribes in Queen Anne's War when he was interrupted by this new and surprising news about the wreck of the *Nottingham Galley.*

It had been three weeks since the judge had arranged to have Captain Deane send his story to his friend Cotton Mather down in Boston when the three crewmen came to him with a new puzzling wrinkle. More than a wrinkle—a whole counter narrative.

Apparently there was even more to this tale than cold, suffering, and cannibalism.

The three men were dead serious—they wanted to tell their side of the story formally under oath. Two of them had signed the captain's protest but now wished to disavow their endorsement of Deane's version of the events, calling the document "false, and Hardly a word of Truth in it."

As a member of Portsmouth's high society, Penhallow was probably predisposed to believing the story of a captain over three men who were "only sailors." But he had developed a reputation as being fair and just, "charitable to the poor and hospitable to strangers." The judge was considered "prompt and firm" and "literally a terror to evil-doers," and he agreed to hear the men out. His curiosity no doubt piqued, he scheduled a deposition hearing for February 9. Penhallow asked Captain Deane to attend as well.

When the date arrived, the crewmen gave Penhallow their written statement and the judge made a formal note:

Christopher Langman, Nicholas Mellin [sic], *and George White, personally appeared before me the Subscriber, one of Her Majesty's Justices of the Peace in the Province of New Hampshire in New England, and Member of Council within the same, this 9th Day of February, 1710-11 and made Oath to the Truth of what is above written, Captain Dean* [sic] *at the time of taking this Oath being present.*

The deposition the three crewmen made was brief—they seemed determined to go on record as soon as their health would allow. And they ended up paying a high price for speaking out against the captain. White was apparently right to be worried about Deane's intentions—even after he signed the protest, just what White had predicted came to pass.

Deane took some of the monies that the people of Portsmouth had donated for the care of the crew and squirreled them away rather than use them for the feeding and care of his men. As Langman put it: "He likewise wrong'd us of what the Good People gave us towards our relief, and applied it to his own and his Brother's Use." A wealthy merchant donated clothing to the men, and Deane intervened again. "When Captain John Wentworth gave several of our Men good Cloaths, Captain Deane came and order'd them the worst that could be had." Eventually the owners of the tavern and the gentle town benefactors had had enough, and they evicted the crew. Deane's behavior, said Langman, was "so barbarous as to get us turn'd out of our lodgings, before we were able to shift for our selves."

Scarcely recovered from their many ailments, without work or worldly possessions, the crew were unceremoniously pushed into the snowy streets. "The Captain had reason indeed to commend the Charity of the Gentlemen of New England," said Langman, Mellen, and White, "we were unhappily deprived of the chief effects of it by the Captain's Brother; who being the person that received it, took care not to be wanting for the Captain and himself, whereas we had nothing but what was fit for such miserable Wretches, who were glad for anything, since we were then uncapable of working for better."

Like Captain Deane's, the full story told by Langman, Mellen, and White would later be published back in England. Their most complete story is told in this later document. A set of separate depositions taken in England and published alongside the account they wrote together occasionally provides some individual nuance, adding distinction to each of the three voices. Their story has been referred to as the "Langman Account," but is better understood as the "Langman, Mellen, and White Account."

The story the three men told the judge was full of conflict, mutiny, betrayal, and raw bloody violence. And it was dramatically different from the tale of a simple maritime accident he'd heard from the ship's captain.

Chapter 11

THE PROBLEMS OF THE *NOTTINGHAM GALLEY* BEGAN EVEN BEFORE SHE shoved off from London. According to Christopher Langman, Nicholas Mellen, and George White, the small galley simply wasn't ready to sail. As the docks bustled around them that August day—the Thames seemed like the center of the universe in 1710, with warships and fishing boats and dories all fighting for space in the crowded river—the crew outfitted the ship for their short voyage to Ireland. As they did so, the three deponents surveyed the situation around them and were not impressed on a number of counts. First was the ship's company itself—the vessel had a crew of fourteen, just as Captain John Deane had said, but able seamen they all were not. According to the trio, "not above 6 of the men were capable to Serve in the Ship, in case of bad Weather." The first mate and the boatswain must have counted themselves among the experienced hands, along with the captain, which left ten others aboard.

Jasper Deane listed his profession as seaman, so it's safe to assume he knew his way around a deck. The "Swede" demonstrated so much competence building the raft on Boon Island that he, too, must have been among the experienced sailors. The "gunner," Christopher Gray, probably had worked his way up through the ranks of common seaman and able-bodied seaman. Miles Whitworth, the cook, the Carpenter, and the ship's boy were not expected to be competent sailors. Which left the remaining three sailors unskilled. Two of these were Charles Graystock, and William Saver. (Langman, Mellen, and White name only the survivors—the last ordinary sailor, who died on the raft with the Swede, remains completely anonymous. According to Captain Deane, it was his body that washed up on the beach at Wells, Maine.)

The first mate and boatswain might have been disappointed in the crew, but in fact it was fairly typical for a merchant ship setting out from London in wartime. Manpower was scarce, and the Royal Navy and the merchant service were in hot competition for every able-bodied seaman. The *Nottingham Galley* was built during an era in which ships were designed to get by with smaller crews, but often it seemed to the sailors manning these vessels that they had to work harder. The grievance of having too few hands aboard was a frequent complaint and sometimes one of the reasons given for mutiny. Club-wielding press gangs tore through the streets and taverns of London forcibly enlisting sailors into the Royal Navy to face poor living conditions, harsh discipline, low pay, and the dangers of combat at sea. Press gangs might have boarded merchant ships returning to London to take sailors right off the decks and send them back out to sea after a long trading voyage—sometimes before the men even had a chance to collect their pay. Not only did impressment drive up the demand for sailors, but it also sent sailors fleeing inland to avoid the gangs, further aggravating the shortage of crewmen. Seamen often signed onto merchant vessels for the sole purpose of escaping the gangs, preferring the money they could make in the private sector over life as a navy man. And there were incentives for the sailors who signed on for the *Nottingham Galley*'s voyage to Boston in 1710. Experienced sailors could make £2.20 per month in wartime as opposed to the usual £1.46. Langman made around £4.38 rather than £3.26, and Mellen earned £3.20 instead of £2.06 in peacetime.

The port of destination, Boston, offered another enticement for common sailors to join the voyage of the *Nottingham Galley*—press gangs were not allowed to operate in the American colonies, where labor was chronically in short supply. In eighteenth-century Boston, rioting mobs and town fathers alike stood against attempts at the impressment of locals because all able-bodied men were needed ashore. If a member of the *Nottingham Galley*'s crew jumped ship upon arrival in Boston, he stood a good chance of finding work and could avoid the potential for being pressed into the Navy upon return. It wouldn't be easy though—even in Boston authorities cooperated in the hunt for sailors gone missing from their ships.

According to Langman, the ragtag band on the *Nottingham Galley* were not competent sailors, nor were they ready to battle the elements. And they were even less prepared for a run-in with the French. The ship may have had ten guns aboard, and one man designated as a gunner, but, as Langman and his two allies pointed out, four of these cannons were "useless," and she was sailing on a long journey during a time of war.

The ongoing conflict was inescapable, truly global in scope and demanding serious consideration in every water through which the *Nottingham Galley* would sail. English merchant ships had to be cautious not only as they moved in European waters but also as they made their way past Maritime Canada toward New England. French corsairs hid in both places, capturing rival vessels.

Captain Deane knew all this, of course. And when the *Nottingham Galley* finally shoved off, she traveled with several other merchant ships in a convoy escorted by two men-of-war, including the HMS *Sheerness*. The ship met the parade at an area near the sandbank at the mouth of the Thames called "the Nore," and they took a position "off of Whitby" on the east coast of England, and "brought to" when a storm blew in.

Then, according to Mellen, White, and Langman, Captain Deane took what appeared to be a calculated risk by breaking from the Navy's protection and making the run up over Scotland past the Shetland Islands to Northern Ireland in what was described as a "fine gale." Since the *Nottingham Galley* was built for fast sailing, leaving the convoy probably didn't seem terribly out of the ordinary at the time. One advantage of the galley-style ship was that it could beat the other merchant vessels into port and get its goods to market first. This is what Deane appeared to be thinking when they left the procession and made haste under full sail to Killybegs, in Donegal County on the northwest coast of Ireland.

Five days after leaving the convoy, Langman, Mellen, and White reported that the *Nottingham Galley* approached "the bay," a small inlet just north of the island of Arranmore, which the English called Aran. They were a little less than a day's sail from Killybegs, to the south in Donegal Bay, when two strange sails were spotted lying in their path. The first mate, the boatswain, and seaman White believed they had run right into the hands of the enemy—French privateers looking for English vessels to sack.

Privateering is often confused with piracy, but these French corsairs were actually buccaneers who flew the flags of their nations. Governments issued "letters of marque and reprisal" that allowed private captains to steal and plunder from the ships of the enemy backed by the full legal authority of the state. It was a practice that dated to the Middle Ages, and through the centuries it grew in sophistication, becoming an entrepreneurial enterprise complete with venture capital. Investors would put up the money to buy and outfit ships, but instead of paying crew members straight wages, they paid shares of the captured treasure—the more these buckos brought back, the more they made.

The French became famous for their skill at privateering—they were feared widely—and their ships were considered the best designed for the job. During the wars that raged between England and France from 1695 and to 1713, French corsairs took ten thousand ships, half to three quarters of which were English. The loss of English merchant vessels peaked in the early years of the war, just after the French navy gave up on the idea of taking on England and Holland in major fleet actions. Rather than meeting the more powerful navies of their adversaries in combat on the open sea, they unleashed their naval vessels to prey on English commerce as privateers, in a sort of partnership between the French state that provided the ships and the private interests who financed their ventures.

Despite the defeats French armies were suffering on land, French privateers continued to operate successfully, terrorizing European waters, the North American coast, the Caribbean and Mediterranean Seas, and beyond. They remained a major threat to English shipping until the end of the war in 1712. The coast of Ireland became a favorite hunting ground of the corsairs because of its proximity to France—and because Ireland's low-priced goods were a constant temptation for English merchantmen. And they were still going strong when the *Nottingham Galley* shoved off from London.

Captain Deane was evidently unconcerned about the two ships that lay in the path of the *Nottingham Galley* and "would have bore down (on them) . . ." claimed Langman, Mellen, and White. To the astonishment of his crew, he seemed ready to either allow the *Nottingham Galley* to be captured or simply refused to admit that they faced a likely enemy.

Then, in half a sentence, these sailors made in their statement before Judge Penhallow an extraordinary declaration for their time and place. They continued, ". . . but the Men would not consent to it, because they perceiv'd them [the two vessels lying ahead] to be French men-of-war."

Judge Penhallow must have found the term *consent* an unusual choice of words. It was not uncommon for a merchant captain to consult with his men when faced with the choice of standing and fighting, running, or surrendering, but eighteenth-century captains didn't need the permission of their crew for anything. A captain's authority was all but absolute. Did Langman, Mellen, and White mean that Captain Deane ordered the sails set to take the *Nottingham Galley* in the direction of the alien ships and his crew refused, or did the captain merely state an opinion in consultation with his crew, and the crew disagreed?

Judge Penhallow certainly understood—anyone with a passing knowledge of maritime history would have—that a ship is not a democracy. In the parlance of the time, anything from a minor questioning of authority to open revolt might be considered "mutiny." Langman, Mellen, and White didn't say that they "convinced" Captain Deane to stay clear of the strange sail. In brief and almost casual terms, Langman, Mellen, and White suggested that the crew was in a state of mutiny, but they passed quickly over that fact in their confession. As first mate it would have been Langman's duty to see that the captain's orders were carried out. Langman states that it was "the men" who would not consent, but he doesn't mention taking any action to make them obey.

The crew of the *Nottingham Galley* not "consenting" to their captain's wishes certainly appears to meet the standard of mutiny. But almost as surprising as Langman, Mellen, and White's admission of disobedience, was Captain Deane's mild reaction. He seems to have simply acquiesced. Deane's response suggests it was indeed nothing more than an ongoing consultation between captain and crew. And perhaps that's all it was, since the disagreement went on as the alien vessels chased the *Nottingham*

Galley "for about the Space of three Leagues," during which time Deane "often would have bore down upon them" if it were not for the objections, or resistance, of "the men."

As if nothing unusual had happened, Langman, Mellen, and White continued their story. "Upon this we stood off to Sea until 12 at Night, when the Captain, coming upon Deck, we Sail'd easily in toward the shore, by the Mate's Advice, 'till Daylight, and came so near land that we were forced to stand off." Here Captain Deane accepted Langman's "advice." Generally it was not so easy to escape from privateers, which were built for speed and had large crews who could quickly change sail, board, and take prizes. But the *Nottingham* was also built to fly, and she had an advantage in shallow waters due to her shoal-shaped hull. The wind direction might have also been favorable. They escaped without incident, hanging to the coastline.

The *Nottingham Galley* wasn't yet home free. Langman, Mellen, and White reported that the "next Day we saw the two Privateers again, and the Captain propos'd to stand down toward them, or to come to." In other words Deane again appeared to want to allow the vessels to overtake the ship or even turn and sail toward them.

The behavior of Captain Deane must have been extremely puzzling to his crew. They'd already outdistanced the two ships once—why should they turn and engage the threat? Was their commander incompetent? Or was something else going on?

To the men of the vessel, it seemed that Deane was deliberately trying to let the *Nottingham Galley* be captured by French warships, even while the owners of the ship and cargo—the captain's brother, "Jasper" Deane, and Miles Whitworth—looked on.

What happened next stunned Mellen. The boatswain testified in his deposition that he was on deck and overheard a conversation between Captain Deane and Whitworth. The merchant told the captain "that he would rather the said Ship would be lost than obtain her design'd Port in Safety, having made £200 Insurance."

Captain Deane responded that "his brother Jasper Deane had made £300 insurance and immediately after said, if he thought he could secure the Insurance he would run the Ship on Shore," a common practice against privateers in an otherwise hopeless situation. The captain then turned to Mellen and ordered him to hoist the tender over the side—to prepare for evacuation.

Seaman White heard the same thing. He noted that he was within earshot on the previous day, when Whitworth had said "that he had rather be taken than not" upon encountering the two suspicious ships. The captain's strange course of action seemed to suddenly become clear—the Deane brothers and Whitworth were trying to perpetrate insurance fraud. Or at least the captain's intentions were clear to Mellen. The boatswain had come to view John Deane as a madman, hell-bent on collecting insurance money even if it meant losing the *Nottingham Galley* on the rocks of Maine.

In an era known more for swashbuckling and piracy, a charge of insurance fraud seems incongruous. But attempts to defraud insurers began almost as soon as the first insurance policies were written. During this particular period a sort of insurance craze was underway. A historian of Lloyd's Coffee House points that one could obtain insurance for just about anything, including truthfulness, marriage, chastity, the long life of horses, or protection from "death by drinking in Geneva." Policies against the loss of ships and cargo at sea were common and readily available, underwritten by stay-at-home gentlemen merchants.

And fraud was easy. At the time it was even described as "prevalent." Buying insurance from multiple sources was simple for captains and businessmen, and the policing and investigation of suspected fraud cases weren't particularly sophisticated. In one noteworthy example before the war with France, a master tried to bribe the pilot with drink as they entered a French port so he'd look the other way when the ship was run aground. A suspicious French official seized the vessel and returned it and its cargo to its owner in England. The colorful trial that followed revealed that the owner had "one way or another taken £3,000 of insurance on £500 worth of goods." In this instance, many of the common sailors testified, though the magistrate struggled to understand their salty dialects and odd mannerisms, making for a comic spectacle.

As Boatswain Mellen prepared their boat for an escape from the *Nottingham Galley*, John Deane and Whitworth went below to pick out the most valuable items to take off the ship. These were put into a chest, and he "commanded the men to carry them into the Boat, which they did."

This time there was no rebellion, at least not initially. The crew's opposition would have threatened any attempt to unlawfully collect on the allegedly over-insured ship and cargo—the complicity of the crew was needed for a fraud scheme to succeed.

Captain Deane no doubt realized what being captured by French privateers would mean to the sailors aboard his ship. He had apparently backed down from his mutinous crew quite easily on the previous day, when they first came upon the strange sails. If the *Nottingham Galley* were taken, his crew members would see practically all of their personal possessions taken—which could amount to a considerable sum

Though sailors occupied one of the lower rungs of English society, they had to come up with a sizable investment just to equip themselves for a career at sea. As one seaman of the period pointed out, men in just this type of situation could lose "more in a moment than they can get again, maybe in all their life time."

A typical sailor would carry aboard multiple changes of clothing, including shirts, a jacket, breeches, stockings, shoes, woolen gloves, a "whapping large watch-coat, cloak or military campaign coat," and a flat, round hat called a "Monmouth cap," or "mountaineers" or "hunters" cap with ear flaps. Unlike the apparel worn by the public at large, a sailor's clothes were often made of canvas or cotton, since these materials were easier to clean and were durable. Mariners did their own mending, which required a needle and thread. Other expenses included bedding—pillows, pillow cases, "rugs," and blankets—and things like razors, penknives, scissors, and snacks to augment their shipboard diet, things like sugar, brandy, cheese, pepper, and mustard. Books, too, were often found in the lockers of seamen.

All of this added up. One sailor of the period claimed that each voyage cost him £5 in "conveniences"—not counting his initial investment in wardrobe—but average monthly wages were £2.20 for common sailors in wartime. Aside from all these personal necessities, sailors on the *Nottingham Galley* probably had items stashed aboard that they intended to trade when they reached Boston. Over pints at taverns in the London neighborhoods of Wapping and Rotherhithe, the crew would have learned of the products in demand in America, and they would likely have tucked away goods as part of their "privilege," to augment their incomes. If captured by the French, all of this would be gone.

And they'd likely be hauled off with it. As common seamen they'd be bound for a French prison to await a prisoner exchange. The taking of ships was such a lively business between the English and French that the system of prisoner swapping was well established, and for officers and gentlemen reciprocity meant that the temporary living conditions in France wouldn't be especially arduous. Indeed, gentlemen prisoners might be given the freedom of the towns in which they were held. Common sailors, on the other hand, wouldn't be so comfortable. Captured English sailors might expect to rot for months in a French prison.

Captain Deane had an alternative to capture. He could plausibly claim that enemy vessels forced him to run the *Nottingham Galley* aground— they drew down on him and in the ensuing chase his ship struck rock. The friendly shores of Ireland would be an ideal location for such a scuttling. Done like this, the Deanes and Whitworth could lose the ship with fewer unfavorable consequences for all involved. As was the tradition in trans-Atlantic voyages, the crew had presumably already received a month's pay at Gravesend. (Crews were paid this portion of their wages after the ship was loaded and underway to keep them from jumping ship while still in port.) This meant that, if the men backed their captain in such a maneuver, they could save most of their valuables and keep at least a month's earnings without making the long and hazardous voyage across the Atlantic. They could be back in London in a week or two—unlike the situation they would have found themselves in if they'd been taken by the French on the open sea the previous day.

On the other hand, if they rebelled against the captain, they risked both punishment and loss of wages. Deane would have felt reasonably secure that his men, faced with these carrots and sticks, would see the merits of his plan—it was clearly in their interest to do so. But to be certain, he decided to sweeten the deal. John Deane was a man who demanded personal loyalty, and in exchange he "promis'd that we should want for nothing," according to Langman, Mellen, and White.

If it were all about interests, Captain Deane's plan should have worked. But it wasn't so easy—sometimes principle gets in the way. During the previous day's encounter with the potentially hostile ships, it was the "men" who wouldn't allow the ship to be taken. This time they apparently didn't raise any objection, willing to go along with their captain. As the boatswain and the other men followed the captain's instructions, they all "plainly saw that he resolv'd to lose the Ship."

For whatever reason, Langman decided he couldn't sit by and watch the captain commit this misdeed. As the men described it: "He [Captain Deane] was opposed by Mate Christopher Langman, who wrought the Vessel through between the Main and an Island, and she arrived safely at Killybags in Ireland that same Night."

Hours of action get compressed into a single sentence. Not surprisingly, Langman, Mellen, and White chose to emphasize Captain Deane's perfidy rather than the mutinous behavior of the first mate. Judge Penhallow no doubt wondered how exactly Langman seized control of the ship. Did he order a change of sail when Captain Deane and Whitworth were below selecting the goods they wanted to bring with them off the boat? How did the captain react? Did Langman simply confront Deane and boldly declare that he was taking over the ship? Did all of the sailors join with Langman, or did some stand with Deane?

The men explained in their written deposition:

The Master the next Day would have gone ashore and left the Ship, and put a Chest and several other things in the Boat. The Mate told him, That he would not consent to any such Thing, for he then saw no Danger in being Taken, and told the said Master, That it was early in the Morning and but Seven Leagues from our Port, and a fair Wind to run along the Shore. The said Master was then heard to say by the Boatswain and several of the Ship's Company, That, if he thought the

Insurance would be Paid, he would immediately run her ashore. So
that we all plainly saw that he was willing to lose the said Ship. The
Mate told him, that if he would, by God's Assistance he might fetch
the Port before Night, if he would make Sail; but if he had a design
to give the ship away, he might. The said Master found that the Mate
was not willing to do what he proposed, and that he could not obtain
his Desire, and made Sail, and about Six or Seven in the Evening we
arrived at our desired Port Killybags . . .

The three sailors kept their description of the drama that ensued short
and free of anger or invective. But hard words must have been spoken on
board, and the situation could easily have escalated to pushing and shov-
ing, the brandishing of weapons, or threats of violence. All this they kept to
themselves. The three deponents surely didn't want to declare the full extent
of their rebellion against the captain—it was after all a form of mutiny,
which was punishable by death. Deane, likewise, wouldn't want to make his
actions or his weaknesses public. So he made no mention of the incident.

To Judge Penhallow, receiving this extraordinary statement, there
wasn't much wiggle room on either side. Langman, Mellen, and White
admitted that members of the crew under Langman's direction behaved
mutinously. But they only did so to prevent Captain Deane from his
apparent attempt to run the *Nottingham Galley* aground to collect insurance money.

Which was worse?

Recorded mutinies were relatively rare—and always dangerous propositions. During the first half of the eighteenth century, nearly sixty instances
were recorded among English sailors, or a little over one per year. But
these were just the cases that were brought before Admiralty Courts or
mentioned in logbooks. Without question there were many more shipboard insurrections that fit the definition of mutiny that the history books
have forgotten.

Sailors of the period had all kinds of motivations for mutiny, including overly harsh or unfair discipline, want of adequate provisions, denial

of shore leave, or simply the presence of a cabal of bad characters among their ranks. In half of all recorded cases, the mutineers were successful in taking control of the ship, and roughly a third of these mutineers turned pirate after overthrowing their commanders. Yet, in spite of the difficult situations found aboard vessels of the time, mutinies usually stemmed from personal animosities and passionate feelings—which meant they often turned violent and murderous.

Harsh penalties made rebels keen to kill anyone who might betray them. Take the case of the *Haswell*, which was on its way to Virginia in 1735 when the boatswain led the crew in an uprising and "murdered the master and his mates in a most barbarous manner." Because of the brutality of the deed, the crew of the *Haswell* were prime candidates to go pirate, which might have been their ultimate plan, but at the French island of Maria Galente, near Guadeloupe, they tried to pass the *Haswell* off as a legitimate trading vessel. Unfortunately for the mutineers, a translator tipped off the governor, and the crew and ship were seized. Three of the men were simply hanged—and they were the lucky ones. The boatswain and another sailor were "broke on the wheel," meaning they were tied to a wagon wheel and slowly turned, their bones breaking one by one as they were clubbed to death with an iron rod.

The best-known mutinies were bloody, but removing the captain from control of a ship could also be nonviolent, as illustrated by cases more analogous to the circumstances claimed by Langman, Mellen, and White. In 1681 the crew of the *Greyhound* refused to sail home from a Mediterranean port without the protection of a convoy "for fear of the Turk." In another example the first mate of the *Edward*, while sailing in Chesapeake Bay in 1669, led the whole crew in taking over the ship when the captain ordered a change of course that the crew felt certain would end in a shipwreck. Undoubtedly there were many more similar unrecorded incidents such as these, in which accommodations were reached; a captain did not want to admit weakness, nor a crew rebellion.

Mutiny usually formed around a nucleus of rebels, and they could succeed with as few as 20 percent of the ship's company participating, so long as the remaining 80 percent were neutral. Langman, Mellen, and

White alone constituted 20 percent of the crew of the *Nottingham Galley*, and they implied that other members of the crew supported them. The participation of the first mate and boatswain, with their shipboard leadership status, was certainly notable in their case.

After Langman's takeover, the *Nottingham Galley* slid up to the docks at Killybegs on the night of August 13, 1710. To an Irish longshoreman overlooking the galley's arrival, everything must have appeared quite routine. The men bustled about the ship preparing it for the docks. The captain and the gentlemen aboard disembarked to pursue their business dealings. Trim and orderly, the small vessel sat while the sea lapped at its hull.

No one ever would have guessed that this was a ship whose crew had mutinied hours earlier against a captain, the owner of the ship, and their merchant ally, who had attempted to execute a plan to commit insurance fraud. For all parties concerned it was best to pretend as if nothing had happened.

According to Langman, Mellen, and White, however, the conflict had only just begun.

Chapter 12

THE *NOTTINGHAM GALLEY* SPENT A LONG TIME IN KILLYBEGS—TOO LONG, some would say. During the ship's stay in port, the crew unloaded and sold whatever goods they had brought to that market from London and then took on the thirty tons of butter and the three hundred cheeses. They likely also brought aboard various last-minute provisions for the crew, such as salted beef and bread, for the long voyage across the Atlantic. While the men were readying the ship, Captain John Deane, his brother Jasper, and Miles Whitworth were off conducting the business. For weeks on end. For forty-one days they sat in this small, out-of-the-way Irish port.

A month is a long time for a trading ship to wait in any port—especially as the season grew late and the difficulties of a North Atlantic crossing mounted. Every day they spent in Killybegs, the autumn breezes picked up, the weather grew colder, winter got closer, and with it came the greater likelihood of squalls and nor'easters. Langman, Mellen, and White offered no explanation for this delay. Perhaps the Deane brothers and Whitworth had trouble locating a cargo. Crew members could have been spooked by the events of the previous day and jumped ship. Searching for replacements would have taken time. But there is no record of any desertions, and neither the captain nor the first mate mentions such a thing.

That any of the ship's company stayed with the *Nottingham Galley* after they and their belongings had nearly been given over to the French enemy is remarkable. Several factors may have contributed to their decisions. Since Captain Deane needed his crew, he probably went to great lengths to assure them he was done trying to lose the ship and its cargo.

It would have been consistent with Deane's style to offer a quid pro quo to Langman and Mellen in which he forgave their rebellion and the first mate and boatswain forswore any knowledge of the captain's attempt at insurance fraud.

For common sailors, their only prospect was to join the crew of another ship in Killybegs that happened to need hands, or to sign on as a passenger back to London and face the press gangs who were conscripting seamen on the streets—not especially likely or promising options. On the other hand, the first mate and boatswain had already shown they wouldn't stand by and watch Captain Deane surrender the ship to the French; perhaps they would intercede again should a similar situation arise. Deane could have looked around to find substitutes, but it was getting late in the season. And they wouldn't necessarily encounter any more privateers. If the *Nottingham Galley* could clear Ireland without incident, she was unlikely to run across French vessels in the broad expanse of the North Atlantic. Only as she drew near French Canada would there again be a real possibility of confrontation.

Because of her long stay in Killybegs, the *Nottingham Galley* would have to move with all speed to complete the journey before cold weather set in. With winter weather, they knew, came exponential increases in hardship and danger. She was built for speed, though, and with any luck she'd arrive in Boston without incident. The scenario was an optimistic one, but not entirely unreasonable. And so the *Nottingham Galley*, apparently with its entire original crew, set sail from Killybegs on September 24.

As the ship shoved off to make the long Atlantic crossing, the crewmen waited to see what Captain Deane would do. Both the first mate and boatswain had been involved in mutiny—not once, but twice. They couldn't continue to sail under the conditions that had prevailed on the voyage to Ireland. The captain simply couldn't allow the kind of insubordination he'd seen thus far. No doubt majority owner Jasper Deane was disgusted with the way the voyage had commenced, and Miles Whitworth was likely nervous about his investment. They knew that for a man of Captain Deane's time, place, and profession, the situation was unacceptable. And for a man of his personality, it was intolerable.

Traditions—and even law—held that once at sea a ship's captain was all powerful. One study of early eighteenth-century merchant sailors states, "The seaman was forcibly assimilated into a severe shipboard regimen of despotic authority, discipline, and control." However, this was apparently not so on the *Nottingham Galley*, which thus far had been governed by the consensus of the crew, according to Langman, Mellen, and White.

By any standard of the day, it was necessary for Captain Deane to reestablish his authority once the *Nottingham Galley* was again at sea. If Deane had deliberately tried to lose his ship, his crew held a legal weapon they could use against him in the admiralty courts. The threat that they might reveal his attempt to defraud the underwriters of the voyage was a serious one. Psychological issues were also in play—Deane's crew had shamed him in front of his own brother, the owner of the ship, as well as Whitworth, the gentleman investor. What manner of a captain was John Deane if he couldn't maintain command of his ship? Jasper Deane may not have explicitly taunted his brother with this question, but it still had to have hung in the air—and reverberated over and over again in John Deane's mind. The captain would have to assert himself with the crew, and in front of the owner and investor, in order to salvage the voyage—and his reputation.

And so he did. Upon leaving Killybegs, Langman, Mellen, and White charged Captain Deane with engaging in a brutal round of corporal punishment. Captain Deane, "by his barbarous Treatment of our Men," they claimed, "had disabled several of 'em." Whatever anger, resentments, and frustrations he had pent up, he unleashed. "Two of our best Sailors were so unmercifully beat by him, because they oppos'd his Design above mentioned, that they were not able to work in a Month."

This sort of harsh discipline was rare on merchant vessels, unlike navy ships, where lashings with cat o nine tails could leave disciplined sailors near death. But if the first part of the story told by Langman, Mellen, and White is true—that Deane tried to lose the ship and the men mutinied—then such beatings were entirely believable. Insolence at sea alone justified corporal punishment. There was no punishment too severe for mutiny.

When discipline was called for on merchant ships, sailors were often confined in "bilboes," long iron bars with shackles fastened to the deck. Long shackling in severe weather could be considered cruel punishment. Beatings with a rope or a cane often followed, though other instruments could be used as well.

Captain Deane's opponents never specified which sailors were beaten, only that they were among the "best sailors." White would be a likely candidate, but he didn't mention the incident in his deposition. The man most guilty of disobedience, Langman, didn't seem to have been disciplined at this time. In fact Captain Deane seemed to have made several attempts to hold on to, or win back, the allegiance of Langman. First mates could and did suffer physical punishment from their captains, but it was very rare and dangerous if the mate had the support of the crew, as in the famous case on the *Bounty*, where First Mate Fletcher Christian was far more popular among the crew than was Captain William Bligh.

Whether or not Boatswain Mellen was beaten is also open to question, but he probably wasn't because his rank would have justified specific mention. On a traditional ship the boatswain would administer the punishment, but Mellen was among the rebels, and it seems Captain Deane himself took the rod to those he punished. This was not out of the ordinary for a ship's captain on a small vessel.

The nature of a captain's authority aboard ship was a personal matter. On a voyage to the West Indies two years later in 1712, English captain Nathaniel Uring suspected that several of his crew were ready to turn pirate. Like a father with misbehaving children, Uring called his crew on deck and beat the men he suspected of fomenting the mutiny one at a time with a cane until he uncovered the plot. So severe was the punishment that Uring reported that its threat kept the crew "exactly diligent and obedient during the rest of the voyage." Captain Deane, like Uring, made the discipline a personal matter, and also like Uring, he must have retained the loyalty of some of the other men on the ship.

Langman, Mellen, and White's accusation that the beaten sailors were thrashed so brutally that they couldn't work for a month was typical of charges pressed in the admiralty courts against abusive captains.

Beatings of this nature were counterproductive and seemed to cross the line from discipline to abuse. After all, if a sailor was physically punished such that he couldn't do his job, then what was the point of the punishment? But it happened. In one especially ugly case, a captain felt a crew member was playing sick. He pulled the man from his hammock "by the hair of his head & told him he would be his Doctor and with great violence gave him upwards of sixty blows over his head, eyes, face, mouth and breast & knocked and beat his head against the cable." The sailor reportedly couldn't work again for two months.

According to the three deponents, Captain Deane's disciplinary measures didn't end with the beatings. "Besides," they claimed, "he put us to short Allowance, so that we had but one Quart of Water per Head in twenty four Hours, and had nothing to eat but salt Beef, which made us so dry that we were forc'd to drink the Rain water that run off the Deck."

According to Langman, Mellen, and White, the drinking water was kept under lock and key while the *Nottingham Galley* and its crew made their slow, storm-tossed voyage across the Atlantic. One sailor, they said, couldn't stand it any longer. Upon finding the hold open, he went below for "a Gallon of water to Quench our Thirst." Captain Deane discovered the attempt and "knocked down" the man, leaving him "for dead."

Deliberate deprivation on board a merchant ship was unusual, but inadequate shipboard sustenance wasn't. And when the master of the ship was part owner, complaints about the low quality and quantity of food were more common, since the more money saved in provisioning the ship, the more money went into the owner's pocket. John Deane wasn't the owner of the *Nottingham Galley*, but his brother was and he was on board, so similar incentives applied. The dissenters said that while the captain "pretended to us that he confin'd himself also to short Allowences yet we knew the contrary" and that he "wanted nothing himself."

With a thirsty, hungry, beaten crew, the *Nottingham Galley* limped across the sea. Captain Deane attributed the ship's slow voyage to "contrary winds," but Langman, Mellen, and White blamed it on the debilitation of a crew riddled with landsmen, weakened by being kept on short allowances, and crippled by the hand of their own captain.

Many unpleasant weeks at sea passed before they finally sailed into the privateer-infested waters off Newfoundland. No sooner had they entered Canadian waters than a ship was sighted in the distance, making for the *Nottingham Galley* "with all the Sail she could." Langman, Mellen, and White claimed that the captain and his allies hoped the oncoming vessel was French, which was a good possibility, as they were now off French-controlled North America. At first glance the two ships appeared evenly matched—they were about the same size—but in fact the *Nottingham Galley* was at a significant disadvantage in a fight against almost any privateer. According to Langman, Mellen, and White, four of the ten guns aboard their ship were "useless," suggesting that Captain Deane was unprepared to defend the *Nottingham Galley* from the very beginning. But it was as much the small size of the crew as the lack of good cannons that made the ship vulnerable in any potential fight.

Primarily used for trade, the galley was a versatile craft capable of carrying out a variety of missions, including combat. It was usually easy to determine what a galley was up to simply by the size of its crew. If it was embarked on a military mission, it would need a crew of 30 or more to man the guns, row, and form boarding parties. Such was the case of the *Illustrious*, a galley with about the same armament as the *Nottingham Galley*, but with a crew of 120 men packed aboard. The *Illustrious* sailed out of Boston to sweep the New England coast for French privateers in September 1711, and it would have needed such a large force of men aboard because each French privateer encountered could be expected to have a company of at least 30 to 40 men apiece.

The *Nottingham Galley* was outfitted for a trading mission, with just enough crew to man the sails, while a privateer opponent would have a deck teaming with gun crews, boarding parties, sharp shooters up in the masts, and plenty of extra men to change sails as needed. Once again the *Nottingham Galley*'s best hope was to run, but this time, unlike their encounters off of Ireland, flight was apparently never even mentioned as an option. It might have been that the winds were unfavorable for escape as the ship bore down on them, or that the captain's harsh disciplinary measures had cowed the crew.

Or perhaps Captain Deane was once again offering his vessel up for capture.

To make certain there was no renewal of rebellion among the crew, Captain Deane apparently chose this moment to end the short allowances. He ordered casks of brandy and beer tapped and invited the crew to drink as much as they wanted. It wasn't hard to bribe a sailor with alcohol—especially after weeks of deprivation. (One notable sea captain of the period said, "Good Liquor to sailors is preferable to clothing.") While the crew was getting drunk, Langman, Mellen, and White claimed that the Deane brothers and Whitworth went below to put on their best clothes, no doubt to look like gentlemen for the French captain who was about to capture their ship.

As it turned out there was no French captain, nor any French privateers. The ship they encountered was the *"Pompey* Galley of London, Captain Den Commander, at which we rejoic'd, tho our Captain was melancholy," according to Langman, Mellen, and White. If so, Captain Den must have been struck by the strange sight aboard the *Nottingham Galley,* with its long-faced captain and his associates dressed as if they were going to a ball in their fine clothes and wigs and the crew staggering around on the deck in drunken celebration.

It was by now early December. Continuing on toward New England, the crew finally sighted land at Cape Sables, the southern tip of Acadia, the future Nova Scotia, which had just been taken from the French by the English. The view of landfall was brief, because bad weather quickly moved in. With the wind blowing hard, Deane is said to have hauled in sail. According to Langman, Mellen, and White, the weather moderated the next day, but instead of keeping on course, the captain ordered the ship to stand away to the north. Langman, Mellen, and White didn't explicitly state the motivation for the dillydallying off Nova Scotia, but they implied that Captain Deane, after his disappointment at meeting the *Pompey,* was hoping to be found by French privateers operating out of Canada. It was a likely spot, since French privateers were known to prey on New England fishermen working the Grand Banks, but the recent English capture of the privateering base at Port Royal may have thrown local French privateers off balance for the short term. By the following spring, however, the *Boston News Letter* would report an English sloop taken by "a large privateer Sloop of 40 men" somewhere in the Gulf of Maine. The article went on to speculate, "Tis very probable the Privateer will continue some time near the Bay of Fundee or Cape Sables, having reserved the Sloop for a Decoy to Fishermen which they expect to meet there."

After some days of circuitous sailing, the *Nottingham Galley* turned south again—right into a menacing cloud. A nor'easter was brewing. As the storm grew worse on the evening of December 10, they were forced to "hand all our Sails and, and lie under our Mizzen-Ballast till Daylight." In the morning Boatswain Mellen had the watch when he sighted land that turned out to be Cape Porpoise, province of Maine—about a dozen miles north of Cape Neddick and Boon Island. Mellen sent word below to Captain Deane.

Both Deane and Langman came up on deck and began to argue. According to Langman and Mellen, the captain baldly stated that this was the first land they had yet seen, "wherein he was justly contradicted by the Mate, which caus'd some Words between 'em: For in Truth we had made Cape Sables a week before." Their exchange became heated, Deane insisting they had just made landfall. If the captain admitted that they had sighted Cape Sables a week earlier, there would have been no good excuse for a week's detour in Canadian Maritime waters. So he pretended they'd just arrived.

The fate of the *Nottingham Galley* seems to have hinged upon that delay. Had they stayed on their original course, "According to the Opinion of the Mate and the Ship's Company, we had, in all probability, arriv'd safe the next Day at Boston."

Chapter 13

OF COURSE THE SHIP NEVER MADE IT TO BOSTON. AND THE CAPTAIN'S falsities and fabrications followed him right off the *Nottingham Galley* and onto the cold, hard shores of Boon Island, according to his accusers. For all the drama he wraps around jumping off the sinking ship and onto the rock—clawing his way desperately onto the island, ripping the fingernails right off his hands, almost getting washed out to sea—the captain didn't garner a scratch as he crawled his way up onto Boon. "(N)ot one Man was hurt in getting ashore," said Christopher Langman, Nicholas Mellen, and George White. Neither did the captain almost drown in his epic escape during the storm-tossed night. The seas washing over the ledge were shallow: "no deeper," according to the three deponents, "than our Middle."

And his fictions went on and on, as far as his three accusers were concerned. The captain didn't know where he was though he says he did; he showed no particular compassion to the cook as he lay dying, though he claims to have nursed him; and when they got around to building a boat, it didn't have a sail and a mast, as the captain claimed. Deane's portrayal of the carpenter as almost no help in the construction of the vessel was inaccurate as well. When they were launching the craft, the three sailors said, "some Controversie happ'd who the six [on board] should be," and the decision seems to have been based on who could best lay claim to the boat. The Carpenter "pleaded his Right" because he built it. He seems to have actually overseen the entire process.

In the Captain's account of the launching, the boat simply capsized and smashed against the rock, but Langman, Mellen, and White report that Mellen, with the help of Grey, the gunner, did everything they could to keep it afloat. The pair "held the Boat almost an Hour with a rope in Hopes to save her till the Weather grew more calm."

When the "Swede" was ready to launch *his* raft, the trio contended that he never asked the captain to accompany him, and the captain made no offer to, saying instead, "Let who will go t'was all one to him." White was the courageous volunteer, and neither he nor the Swede was helped onto the raft by Captain Deane. When the raft overturned, Deane didn't, as he claimed, swim out to rescue White or anyone else. White returned to the rock under his own power and wisely elected not to make another attempt. It was the unnamed sailor who joined the Swede, only to freeze to death upon reaching the mainland.

In his version of the events on Boon Island, Deane cast himself as far and away the healthiest of the shipwrecked company—almost heroically so. He was always busy searching for food for his men and tending to their needs. Langman, Mellen, and White didn't dispute the captain's relative health, but they did suggest that there were others—sailor White himself—who were equally vital. It was White, they say, and not Captain Deane, who first discovered the mussels at low tide and returned to fetch them.

"Tis likewise false, that the Captain went several times out to look for Provisions, for George White was always with him. Nor is it true, that the piece of Cow's Hide before mention'd was brought into the Tent by the Captain's order, for George White brought it without his knowledge."

Most of the discrepancies the deponents found in Captain's Deane story—as the ship's company struggled to survive on the island—were rather minor, and some might be attributed to fatigue and memory loss—or perhaps worse. There was the curious episode when the clouds finally cleared and the men got a look at their surroundings. Langman, Mellen, and White reported that they "could see Houses on the main Land, and several Boats rowing to and fro, which rejoic'd us very much." In his account Captain Deane makes no mention of this stunning fact, that they could actually see civilization from where they were stranded. Here were houses with warm fires and food cooking in them, and boats coming out into the water, which the castaways could actually see, taunting them in their miserable condition. How could Captain Deane fail to report this aspect of their experience on Boon Island?

Cold and hypothermia frequently lead to hallucination. Two Danish soldiers in Greenland found themselves in a deep freeze, suffering severe frostbite on their feet, and they convinced themselves that they were part of a survival experiment that would soon be called off. In this case the vision was a sort of psychological coping mechanism. In another example cold and tired sailors floating in the Pacific after the sinking of their ship imagined that they were still on board and hallucinated that they could see an island close by. Their dementia was so compelling that they took off their life jackets and died trying to swim to the imaginary island. Worse, some sailors from the same group believed they were still under attack and fought and killed each other in the night.

Given the possibility of such vivid cold and fatigued-induced visions, it's quite easy to imagine the castaways on Boon Island seeing distant houses or small boats in the water. What Langman, Mellen, and White saw was a mirage, a hallucination—Boon Island is too far from the mainland to make out men rowing dories. Captain Deane's relative health kept him from sharing their delusions.

For the majority of their time on the island, however, the men had their wits about them. The longer they were marooned, the larger—and more important—became the lies in the captain's story. The three sailors knew that the aspect of their ordeal that would attract the most attention was the eating of the Carpenter, and they pointed out that the captain deliberately changed the facts in his telling to hide his transgressions. It was Captain Deane, they said, who first proposed cannibalizing the Carpenter, arguing "It was no Sin, since God was pleas'd to take him out of the World, and that we had not laid violent Hands upon him." And the captain was hardly bothered by the act of eating a human entrée, they said. "[T]he Captain's Pretensions of being moved with Horror at the Thoughts of it, are false, for there was no Man that eat more of the Corps than himself."

The three deponents claimed that the morning after they refused to eat the Carpenter's carcass, Deane approached them with a piece of the liver "and intreated 'em to eat of it"—like the Devil offering up some evil communion. The captain seems to have been trying to make the mate and boatswain complicit in his own designs to make sure everyone—especially the ranking members of the crew—joined him in the controversial act of man eating.

After taking their macabre meal, the men became so craven and devilish, according to the captain, that he had to haul the remainder of the meat off and stand guard over it, lest they sneak to the Carpenter in the night to feed. "I found they all eat abundance and with the utmost greediness, so that I was constrain'd to carry the quarters farther from the Tent, (quite out of their Reach) least they shou'd prejudice themselves by overmuch eating, as also expend our small stock too soon."

This, according to the trio, was untrue as well. There were no attempts on the meat. "It was likewise false," they said, "that any of the men removed the Dead body from the place where they laid it at first." Gunner Christopher Gray had been present when the butchering was done, and he was witness to the disposal of the remainder of the carcass. The skin, head, and hands—the most human-looking parts—were not reverently deposited into the ocean to be swept away as the captain claims, but were dumped to the side and left on the island as refuse. And there they sat.

As he stood sentinel, Deane claimed he worried about what would happen when their supply of flesh ran out. "This, together, with the dismal prospect of future want, oblig'd me to keep a strict watch over the rest of the Body, least any of 'em shou'd (if able) get to it, and this being spent, we be forc'd to feed upon the living: which we must certainly have done, had we staid a few days longer."

The captain didn't have to beat off devils looking for more flesh, and he didn't have to police the crew to make sure they refrained from gorging themselves. "Nor is there any more Truth in the Care which the Captain ascribes to himself, in hindring us to eat too much of the Corps lest it should prejudice our Health; for we all agreed, the Night before we come off; to limit our selves, lest our Deliverers should be detain'd from coming to us."

The remainder of the meat was allotted to the company on the third of January, this time part of a final cookout. Langman, Mellen, and White reported that the castaways "kept a great Fire, which was seen on the Shore, and proved very comfortable to us, both for its Warmth, and by Broiling part of the Dead Corpse, which made it eat with less Disgust."

After they had all eaten part of the Carpenter, Langman, Mellen, and White said, it wasn't the attitude of the crew that changed, as the captain asserts, but his own. In Deane's account the men became feral and unhinged. "I found (in a few days) their very natural dispositions chang'd," he explained, "and that affectionate, peacable temper they had all along hitherto discover'd totally lost; their eyes staring and look-ing wild, their Countenances fierce and barbarous, and instead of obey-ing my Commands (as they had universally and readily done before) I found all I coul'd say (even prayers and entreaties vain and fruitless) nothing now being to be heard but brutish quarrels, with horrid Oaths and Imprecations . . ."

Deane's opponents deny all this. Instead they say it was he who turned. It wasn't the members of the crew who lost their Christian tem-perance but the gentlemen from Nottinghamshire. "All the Oaths we heard were between the Captain, his Brother and Mr. Whitworth, who often Quarrel'd about their Lying and Eating." (By "Lying" they presum-ably refer to a struggle for place and position in the crowded confines of the tent.)

Not only did his mouth go foul, but so did his very character. The puritanical Langman was offended. "Whereas the Captain often went to Prayers with us before we had the Corps to eat, he never, to our hearing, pray'd afterwards, but behav'd himself so impiously, that he was many times rebuked by the Mate and others for Profane Swearing."

Everyone seemed to agree that the consumption of human flesh cor-rupted the souls of those who engaged in the beastly act.

But it was all souls.

Chapter 14

CAPTAIN JOHN DEANE LOOKED ON HORRIFED AS JUDGE SAMUEL PEN-
hallow listened to the story told by Christopher Langman, Nicholas Mellen, and George White, his world starting to spin around him. According
to the deponents he "had not the Face to deny it, his Character appeared
in a True light, and he was covered with Shame and Confusion." The
tale these common sailors told was a devastating blow to Deane's reputation, which was already in danger due to his behavior in Portsmouth. His
prowess as a man of the sea was questionable, thanks to the wreck. He'd
behaved in a boorish manner with his hosts, the Furbers. Now, before one
of the most noteworthy gentlemen in the colony of New Hampshire, the
very core of his character was also revealed as suspect. The story must have
given Samuel Penhallow pause, and if there was one man in Portsmouth
who could truly damn Deane's reputation, it was the magistrate. Not only
was Penhallow among the most important men in the colony, but he had
a direct line of communication with the single most influential man in all
of New England—Cotton Mather.

The famous Puritan minister had been extremely interested in the
wreck of the *Nottingham Galley*, requesting a timely and reliable account
to publish alongside his popular sermon as soon as possible. Not to be
confused with the brief and legalistic "protest," Mather asked his friend
the judge for a compelling narrative that could move men's souls. And
Deane delivered it, writing and sending a long and detailed account. Captain Deane dated his *Narrative*, "Boston, NE [New England], Jan 26,
1710," which would have been just a few weeks after the ship's company
landed at Portsmouth, but it was not until the beginning of March that
Mather even acknowledged receiving it.

"A remarkable Relation of Distress undergone a Deliverance received by some Sea-faring People is putt into my Hands," he wrote in his diary on March 4. Mather promised himself that he would "endeavor the publication of it in such a manner as may not only glorify the Power, and Wisdome and Goodness of God; but also do good, especially among that sort of people."

But his plan took a pause. A reading of the minister's diary shows him pulled in many directions during that winter and early spring. As usual he carried the weight of eternity on his shoulders for the many souls he encountered during the course of his work. Within his congregation and community there were dead children to be mourned, widows requiring assistance, and wicked church members to be reformed. He pledged, in true Christian fashion, to help a merchant who had wronged him without that man learning the source of the aid. At midwinter his focus shifted from helping seamen to helping orphans. And his own children needed to be guided along the path to heaven. He vowed to spend more time with them, or at least buy one an appropriately edifying book. A promising relationship appeared between Mather's ministry and the University of Glasgow, which required his attention. Many in his flock, he recorded in his diary, experienced great losses at sea, both human and financial, at the hands of French privateers. Then he fell sick.

All of this might have distracted Mather from publishing the captain's account of the *Nottingham Galley* shipwreck. But maybe, too, the depositions left by the captain's opponents made the moralist in him think twice.

Portsmouth was just as busy as the minister. A colonial New England town in winter and at war, the frontier community must have seen the conflict among the survivors of the *Nottingham Galley* as a macabre sideshow. Despite the cold the port on the Piscataqua bustled. On January 22, the *Boston News Letter* reported that "hard weather by Frost, Snow and Thaw hindered the posts" but that the mast fleet, delivering one of the most important of the colony's exports, was ready to depart. In fact wintery conditions kept the ships bearing England-bound pine masts at the dock for about another month—the merchant convoy left in late February.

Meanwhile search-and-destroy missions were being dispatched to hunt down native inhabitants. A Captain Preble returned in mid-February with a small army. In March, Captain Walton, with two hundred men, sailed up to Casco Bay to "St. George's River to drive the Indians from fishing & fowling which is their support this season of the year." Two families consisting of eight persons were "destroyed" except two children, a "Squa," and an Indian who surrendered. The English colonists showed no mercy to the native inhabitants. After so many years of war, the goal was to eliminate the enemy entirely.

With the day-to-day life of Portsmouth spinning around them, the men of the *Nottingham Galley* were left to fend for themselves. Langman, Mellen, and White never said how the crew got by after their eviction from the tavern, but they reported receiving "encouragement" from local folk, who urged them to make lives for themselves in the colonies or to ship out with local captains. Many members of the ship's company were quite literally trying to simply get on their feet, trying to learn how to live and work with new physical disabilities. Some would discover how to tie knots with a missing finger or two, and keep balance on fewer toes. Many failed to retain the "perfect use" of their arms and legs. When spring came at last, several of the *Nottingham Galley* mariners answered the call of the sea once again, taking up the invitation to work on local ships, "some sailing one way and some another," remembered a cheerful Captain Deane.

The remainder of the crew would find passage back to London. It's quite likely that all of the principal parties in the controversy surrounding the wreck of the *Nottingham Galley* had left New England by May 6, since it's around that date when Mather eventually published the first edition of Deane's story. The manuscript was filled with the same tale that the captain had told Penhallow— he'd circulated a draft version among the gentlemen of Portsmouth before sending it on to Boston—bringing his side of the dark affair to a wide audience.

Mather had apparently believed that a controversy would undermine the message he wanted to present and that it was better to wait for all parties to move on before publication. In the end he concluded that it didn't matter who, if anyone, was telling the truth—God would sort the truth out in His time. The point was "to make a Good Use of much Evil occurring in the World, and especially of the strange Punishments inflicted by God on many sinners in the World, and most especially of the Things befalling the Sea-faring Tribe."

Mather tacked Deane's narrative on to the end of the published version of the sermon he gave back in December: *Compassions called for: An essay of profitable reflections on miserable spectacles. To which is added, A faithful relation of some late, but strange occurrences that call for an awful and useful consideration. Especially, the surprising distress and deliverances of a company lately shipwrecked, on a desolate rock, on the coast of New-England.*

By late spring the Deanes and their accusers were all back where they started, in London, the booming metropolis of a burgeoning empire. What a different world it was from Portsmouth. At the time London was arguably the greatest city anywhere, with between 575,000 and 600,000 inhabitants living in its environs. The only city that might come close was Paris, but the war had taken its toll on France, and Louis XIV's bureaucracy bled his kingdom of its economic prowess. By 1711, France was economically exhausted. The heart of the English world, by contrast, pumped out wealth throughout the lengthy conflict. The English countryside continued to supply London with agricultural produce, coal, and other raw materials in exchange for finished products and imported goods from all over the world, including smuggled French wine, which was available in abundance. As the former castaways arrived in London, they would have found the Thames jammed with ship traffic. Only Amsterdam could compare as a world port.

London was also the vibrant political and intellectual center of English civilization. Of the two hundred thousand people living within the city's boundaries, twelve thousand were rate payers with the political franchise. England was by no means a democracy, but parliamentary sovereignty, heated debates between Whig and Tory, and a vigorous press that was relatively free for its time gave politics a popular intensity. Much of the debate at the time centered on religion, including the privilege of the Anglican Church and the rights of dissenters. The arguments ranged from the streets to the taverns to the pages of books. Most of the growing publishing trade was of a religious nature, but this was also the London of Daniel Defoe and Jonathan Swift, pioneers of the novel and authors of, respectively, *Robinson Crusoe* and *Gulliver's Travels*, tales of shipwreck and adventure (and cannibals, in the case of *Crusoe*).

The upper crust of London drank in the town's heady political and intellectual life, entertained each other in stylish homes, attended London's many theaters, socialized in coffeehouses, and retreated to their country estates to escape a city that was growing increasingly crowded and was already being choked by the pollution of thousands of coal fires. Into this fashionable London, John and Jasper Deane and Miles Whitworth—the gentleman of the *Nottingham Galley*—disembarked. Unlike the Deane brothers and Whitworth, who purchased passage back to England, Langman, Mellen, and White had worked their way home.

Another very different London festered alongside this world of gentility. A massive segment of the city's population lived in squalor and disease caused by poor sanitation, inadequate diet, and overcrowding. Most of these residents lay beyond the reach of education, religious institutions, philanthropy, or even the law. They found their entertainment on the streets and in taverns where gin was beginning to replace ale as the preferred drink, the negative consequences of which would be illustrated in William Hogarth's many darkly humorous and moralizing engravings. For these downtrodden people, life in London was a sort of urban version of Thomas Hobbs's state of nature: "nasty, brutish, and short."

A large middle class of artisans and shopkeepers bridged the two Londons, adding necessary social cohesion and charting a difficult though not impossible route to social advancement. While Langman and Mellen might have had their feet in middle-class London at times, the common sailors of the *Nottingham Galley* took their place among the other seamen in the impoverished masses.

The Deane brothers knew that their adversaries were also back in town. And they were keen to prevent the damage done to their reputations in

New England from spreading like a cancer through London society. John Deane's first instinct was to make a deal, to wield carrots and sticks to get what he wanted. On the ship he had used force; this time he decided to make an offering. Surely there was something he could give Langman, Mellen, and White to keep them quiet and get them to support a mutually acceptable version of their harrowing experience together.

The captain wanted to publish a new version of his story for the London audience, and he didn't want his former shipmates to cast doubt upon it. Maybe, too, he worried that the version Mather would publish might contain unflattering language, which would surely find its way to London. It would be prudent to issue an edition over which he had full control—to establish the correct story in England as soon as possible. And he wanted to recast the *Narrative* for the sophisticates of the city anyway. John Deane was no Puritan and did not want to sound like one. Phrases like "seeing the mercy of God in the midst of Judgment" and any references to psalm singing were absent from the version Deane published in London. Langman might have approved of such pious notions and practices, but they wouldn't go down well in the fashionable Anglican world of London, where many gentlemen were already preferring a less personal and less judgmental "Divine Providence."

The captain wasn't thinking of publishing to ease his difficult financial straits, but rather he wanted to protect and promote his reputation, and to a lesser extent, that of his brother (which, of course, would lead to future wealth). That was the plan, and winning over Langman, Mellen, and White would help secure that end. Given the amount of bad blood spilled between them, the idea of Deane pacifying his opponents stretches the imagination. But he seems to have believed that every man, like himself, was driven by his interests, and rationally speaking, Langman, Mellen, and White had nothing to gain by continuing their opposition.

All the time they spent together on the rock, and all those months of winter confinement in colonial Portsmouth, must have given John Deane some insight into the thoughts and behavior of his former shipmates. At least he thought he had an idea of what rankled Langman, Mellen, and White the most about his characterization of events. So Deane, perhaps with his brother, made three significant changes in the text regarding Langman, and to a lesser extent Mellen and White.

First, the captain decided to portray the first mate in the most flattering light he could, making him out to be the hero on the night of the wreck. After the masts had fallen, Deane writes in his new version, "One of the men went out on the Boltsprint, and returning, told me he saw something black ahead, and wou'd adventure to get on shore, accompanied with any other Person; upon which I desir'd some of the best swimmers (My Mate and one more) to go with him, and if they recover'd the Rock, to give notice by their Calls, and direct us to the most secure Place."

No mention is made here of crawling out onto the mast that fell onto the rock. Implicitly, Langman and his allies jumped off the bow of the ship into the raging surf, risking their lives in order to save the rest of the ship's company. The anecdote suggests madness more than heroism. Voluntarily plunging into an icy ocean roiling in great waves and pounding against nearby rocks, as part of a sort of aquatic reconnaissance party, defies common sense. It is the last desperate action a sailor might take before the ship went completely under, but the *Nottingham Galley* was still whole enough that Deane could claim that his next action was to go belowdecks for money, the ship's papers, and gunpowder. Waiting to see if the ship would hold together—an approach that Langman, White, and Mellen suggest most of the ship's company actually took—makes far more sense.

Langman later denied this anecdote, noting that he didn't even know how to swim. Why did Captain Deane feel the need to invent this strange story? Most obviously, by casting them as heroes, the passage flattered Langman and his allies, but it also made liars out them if they endorsed it, which fits a pattern. Just as Deane had tried to make his first mate and crew complicit in his apparently fraudulent activities off the coast of Ireland, and turn them to fellow cannibals in eating the Carpenter on Boon Island, so now he sought to have them join him as authors of an embellished narrative designed to serve their mutual benefit. No one on board would sink their own lifeboat.

The second major edit in Deane's new *Narrative* put Langman on record as forcefully arguing against the wisdom of the "Swede" and a companion making the fatal journey on his raft. Langman's opposition is described as at least as strong as Deane's to what was in fact a suicidal attempt at escape. Again, on this point, Deane's characterization falls into line with his opponents, at least as far as Langman's position is concerned.

And finally—and most important—Deane made his opponents reluctant cannibals, underscoring their religious objections to the act of man eating. It was dangerous ground for him to tread—drawing a distinction would only shed light back on him. It was one thing for rough sailors, with reputations as heathens anyway, to turn cannibal, but could a true gentleman ever eat another human being? And if he did, could he ever be looked upon as a true gentleman again, or would he be hence forward tainted as a brute? Deane evidently felt confident enough to disclose the cannibalism that took place on Boon Island because he believed a significant portion of the public would not condemn him or his desperate act. But he may have been unprepared for the public censure he received.

Deane evidently felt that he passed over the issue of cannibalizing the Carpenter too lightly in his first written accounts of the wreck—or perhaps it became obvious that the reading public hungered for more on the subject—and he elaborated in yet another revised version many years later. This time he pointed out that it was Miles Whitworth, the tender and genteel merchant, who first proposed cannibalism. If "Mr. Whitworth, a young Gentleman, his Mother's darling Son, delicately educated" amid "great an Affluence" could suggest eating the Carpenter, then their circumstances were surely dire enough to countenance something so ghastly. Whitworth was not in fact an especially young man, but he did unquestionably possess the social status of a gentleman. The idea of "converting the Humane Carcass into the matter of their Nourishment" was quickly seconded by a majority of the other starving members of the party, who "urged their Desires with irresistible Vehemence," wrote Deane.

Captain Deane recorded in this later edition of his *Narrative* that he passively listened to the arguments and pleadings of his fellow castaways with an "invincible Silence," and he claims that he was only brought to the gruesome task after the others prevailed upon him with "incessant Prayers and Tears."

In this version of his story, the point is made clear that Deane may have been forced to make an impossible decision, but Langman, Mellen, and White wanted no part. Deane reasoned that it wouldn't hurt to distinguish his own reasoned Christianity from Puritanical irrationality, which the very next morning gave way to hunger anyway. His addition to his *Narrative* is again consistent with what Langman, Mellen, and White also reported. The trio objected to cannibalism on religious grounds, refusing the offer of meat the first night, but gave in and began eating human flesh the next morning.

Jasper Deane, who was perhaps a little less offensive to Langman, Mellen, and White than his brother, arranged to meet with the three dissenters somewhere in London, presumably a tavern or maybe a coffee-house, to discuss these matters. In fact, Jasper Deane seems to have been the sole representative of his and his brother's interests in London at the time. As the owner of the ship, the supercargo, and the older of the two, Jasper Deane may have perceived himself as in charge on land, but it also appears his brother was away on business.

Langman agreed to the meeting, and he arrived with one of his shipmates in tow. Jasper Deane brought along the revised *Narrative*. Langman and his colleague began reading the captain's story, but they didn't get very far before they started raising objections.

And the old conflict was new again.

As onlookers watched, the pair told Jasper Deane just what they thought of him, his brother, and their tale. "Two of us did positively refuse it in publick Company," Langman, Mellen, and White said, "after reading a part of it, and told him to his Face *that it was not true.*"

Had the Deane brothers simply left well enough alone, the three sailors could have had their little revenge and last word in the distant colony of New Hampshire, an ocean away. Merchants plying their trade between North America and the mother country might have repeated the rumors of mutiny associated with the shipwreck, but the only published account at this time was Deane's, the one mildly and not unfavorably edited by Cotton Mather to accompany his sermon. Quite possibly the Deane brothers were unaware that Mather had even published his *Narrative*, as perhaps no copy had yet to reach London. The horrible affair might have died back in New England where it started, becoming the sort of legend that seamen told each other as they sailed past the island. And there were other ports of call that the Deanes could trade with.

But the brothers persisted. Perhaps they were fearful that, given Mather's relationship with Penhallow, the *Narrative* might arrive in London with Langman, Mellen, and White's accusations printed alongside the captain's story. Or maybe John Deane again miscalculated, thinking he could win over his crew, just as he had tried to do before as they approached the mysterious ships off Ireland.

Whatever the reason, the Deanes badly misplayed their hand and the meeting with their opponents only inflamed them, pouring sea salt into wounds that might have healed. After seeing part of the new *Narrative*, Langman, Mellen, and White were again moved to take action. Since Portsmouth the trio had "Apprehensions" that John Deane might misrepresent matters when they were all back in London. It squared with his character. Which is why, they contend, they had refused "the Encouragement which was offered to us in New England," unlike some of the others. Rather than accept job offers aboard ships in Portsmouth, they returned home. After their meeting with Jasper Deane it seemed certain that John Deane was ready to publish this second edition in London.

Langman, Mellen, and White had had enough of the captain and his fabrications. He was a dishonorable man; his actions had killed four men, led others to the most barbarous act possible, and left the lot of them poor wretches with missing fingers and toes, not to mention nightmares. They refused to let him get away with it.

And they resolved to strike first.

Chapter 15

WHAT WAS AN AGGRIEVED SAILOR TO DO? THE USUAL WAY FOR SEAMEN to get satisfaction from their captains was in the admiralty courts, the jurors of maritime affairs. The courts were often effective and a credit to the English judicial system. Christopher Langman, Nicholas Mellen, and George White didn't take this route for a variety of reasons. Sailors typically leveled charges when they felt they were cheated out of wages. In the case of John and Jasper Deane and the *Nottingham Galley,* there was little if any money for which to sue, and the ship was destroyed in a storm. The trio could accuse Captain Deane of physical abuse, but the witnesses were either dead or hopelessly scattered. Whatever charges they decided to level, Langman, Mellen, and White almost certainly lacked the financial resources to wage a court battle.

Instead they scraped together what little money they had to make a new set of depositions in London, lest the ones sworn to in a distant colony lacked sufficient weight. The trio had nothing to gain from spending their meager resources this way—other than some satisfaction for the wrongs they perceived were done to them. They didn't want to see other sailors treated this way, and they certainly didn't want Deane to be perceived as the hero that he cast himself as. Once again they swore under oath that their statements were the truth, made copies, and, according to the Deane brothers and Miles Whitworth, "industriously spread abroad" the depositions.

Abroad here meant one sort of space in particular: the London coffeehouses, which were the very center of English social life and public information. By the eighteenth century, as many as five hundred coffeehouses were situated around London, mostly in areas inhabited by the wealthy and middle class. Coffee and the institution of coffeehouses were first brought home to England by merchants from Ottoman and Muslim Smyrna. These neighborhood cafes offered the sociability of the tavern without the intoxication. And they were spread throughout the entire kingdom and the colonies, becoming crucial nodes of public communication. Most featured a table in some prominent place on which lay, as one Tory observer derisively commented, "a crowd of idle pamphlets." (Coffeehouses were associated with republicanism and distrusted by conservatives.) Most readers couldn't afford to buy newspapers and pamphlets, which in relative terms were very expensive, but literature was available for free reading at the coffeehouse, where it could be consumed along with a stimulating beverage. Covering all manner of topics, these papers were imported from all over the world, and they prompted much discussion and debate.

Some coffeehouses even became broadcast centers, where fresh news was read aloud, sometimes before it went to the presses. One of the best-known cafes, Lloyd's, famously pioneered the use of a pulpit for this purpose. During wartime, of course, the news took on greater urgency, with patrons anxiously awaiting the outcome of battles or word of how their investments fared. Many respectable London gentlemen kept regular hours at their favorite shops, and a few even had their own seats, though coffeehouses were noted for their egalitarian nature.

Beyond the common characteristics of hot beverages and a table containing literature, coffeehouses became specialized. The poets met over at Will's or Tom's near Covent Gardens. Lawyers met near the Inns at Court at the Grecian or at Nando's. Printers and booksellers gathered at the Chapter Coffee House on Paternoster Row, where they had their offices and shops. The politicians, too, had their own preferred coffee shops, with the Whigs meeting at James' Coffee House and the Tories at the Chocolate House (since coffee was for Whigs and republicans, Tories evidently drank chocolate instead). Some had religious affiliations, and, at the other extreme, some were actually thinly disguised brothels where the serving girls offered something more stimulating than caffeine.

The depositions made by the three men of the *Nottingham Galley*, written by hand, would necessarily have had a small distribution, but strategically placed, could still make a large impact. To reach the audience who mattered most to their cause, the merchant community, the trio needed to place their depositions on the tables of only three London coffeehouses, Jonathon's, Garroway's, and Lloyd's, all gathered near— practically extensions of—the Royal Exchange in Cornhill, which was quite possibly the greatest single marketplace in the world. Here traders gathered together from all over the globe to conduct all manner of business, from retail and wholesale selling, to shipping, insurance, and stock trading. Walking past the stately columns at the entrance, visitors gazed upon a grand courtyard full of merchants from every nation, each of which had its own quarter. Businessmen dressed in colorful clothing that reflected their wealth and nationality buzzed in conversation or bustled from meeting to meeting, dodging around the royal statues that decorated the space. In the corners of the courtyard, stairs ascended to access long crowded walkways lined with salesmen hawking the most luxurious goods from all over the world. More stalls bordered the exterior of the exchange, and they extended onto major streets and into various alleyways. The business continued right into the coffeehouses, located in Exchange Alley, or on Lombard Street, where agreements were made and auctions held "by inch of candle." Printers and booksellers, too, were nearby on Paternoster Row.

The London court of public opinion that would try the case of Captain John Deane essentially encompassed these few blocks. The goal was to get all these people talking.

Sailors—and anyone else with a gripe to air—had long understood the power of the coffeehouse. In 1673, letters from common seamen critical of their officers found their way onto literature tables after an indecisive battle at sea, embarrassing the government. Perhaps somewhat gleefully, Langman, Mellen, and White strolled through the crowd of merchants and into Jonathan's, Garroway's, and Lloyd's, where they dropped off their depositions at the various tables and waited to see the reaction.

About ten days later a classified advertisement appeared in the *London Gazette,* which announced "this day is published, *A Narrative of the*

Sufferings, Preservation and Deliverance of Capt. John Deane and Company in the Nottingham Galley *of London, cast away on Boon Island near New England, December 11, 1710."* The story was "Sold by S. Popping at the Black-Raven in Pater Noster-row, and the Printing Press under the Royal Exchange in Cornhill." The price was only 3d, an unusually small sum, suggesting that the pamphlet was subsidized by its publishers, John and Jasper Deane.

With the story of Langman, Mellen, and White also circulating, Jasper Deane—and it seems Jasper was working alone at the time, his brother still off on business—probably felt he couldn't allow the charges to go unanswered. The damage that could be done to the reputation of himself and the captain, with gentlemen merchants discussing the accusations and implications of the depositions over their coffee, was huge. But he had a problem. The only version of the *Narrative* he had to tell their side of the story was the one he had presented to Langman, Mellen, and White in person—the same *Narrative* that showed First Mate Langman in a favorable light.

Astonishingly, Jasper Deane decided to go to press anyway, despite the portrayal of Langman as a loyal and even heroic first mate. The type may well have already been set in the Jasper Deane–edited version of his brother's *Narrative* when the depositions of the seamen appeared in public. Revising the manuscript would have cost too much money—and even worse, too much time. Given the legal and public stands that Langman, Mellen, and White had made in Portsmouth—and their recent rebuff of the new proposed *Narrative*—publishing anything that gave the first mate any credibility at all seems extremely foolish from a tactical point of view. John Deane would not have made such a mistake.

What was Jasper Deane thinking? Did he, to some extent, share Langman's point of view? As later events would suggest, Jasper Deane's strange inertia as the "editor" of John Deane's *Narrative* almost seems a passive-aggressive action against his own brother. At some level Jasper Deane probably blamed the captain for the loss of the ship that he owned and condemned him for the terrible experience on Boon Island. At one point Langman, Mellen, and White noted that of their three opponents—the

Deane brothers and Whitworth—only John Deane was "acquainted with all the Matter of Fact" during their travails. Jasper Deane, probably sleeping soundly in his berth as his rocking ship was steered toward its doom, doesn't seem to have been consulted regarding the *Nottingham Galley's* course during the hours leading up to the wreck.

Perhaps Jasper Deane knew full well that during the voyage—especially on the night of the wreck— Langman showed good judgment and sound conduct, in contrast to his brother. Jasper Deane's emotions were raw, and consciously or not, his public relations strategy was poorly considered. Or maybe Jasper Deane was simply too dim a beacon for such a rocky bit of coast. For whatever reason, instead of revising the *Narrative*, Jasper simply tacked on a postscript that contained their best case against the points laid out in Langman, Mellen, and White's incendiary depositions. If publishing the only account Jasper had in his possession, written in his brother's hand, inadequately defended brother John, so be it.

Captain Deane's *Narrative* was printed by R. Tooke, a printer who regularly worked with bookseller S. (Sarah) Popping. They were part of group of associates who included the well-known John Dunton, at times a "publisher, whole sale, retail and 2nd hand bookseller, auctioneer, journalist and hack." Ideologically, Dunton was a Puritan and a Whig; his associates could be expected to hold similar perspectives. Daniel Defoe, in many ways a kindred spirit to Dunton, was also at times published by Sarah Popping. It cannot be known exactly why the Deane brothers, or Jasper Deane, brought their manuscript to this particular group, but Dunton was personally acquainted with Cotton Mather. Perhaps Mather had suggested to Deane that he try this course, or the Deanes might have perceived some advantage in associating themselves with a Puritan printer, especially if they believed that Mather was going to publish a version of their *Narrative* that included information not favorable to them.

Published in pamphlet form the new *Narrative* was distributed throughout London via hawkers or "mercury traders," men and women who sold printed material on the streets and in the coffee circuit. These hustlers would "cry papers about the streets," calling or singing out, sometimes in verse, often luridly and without regard to accuracy, the nature of the news and literature they sold. A contemporary noted that one particular hawker had a "peculiar happiness of misnaming, wrestling, and commenting upon almost everything she carries."

The mercury traders existed on the margins of society and usually couldn't even read what they sold. Often disabled, occasionally arrested for vagrancy, they were not so much advertising but often the principle source of news for the illiterate masses. And it isn't hard to imagine them happily announcing, to all ears within shouting distance, Captain Deane's frigid shipwreck story of freezing flesh, cannibalism, and creeping madness. In this case there was little need to embellish. The grim survival story and shocking tale of taboo surely created a sensation.

But there was also the matter of that other pamphlet. The defense of John Deane, Jasper Deane, and Miles Whitworth against the charges made in the depositions was raised in their postscript, written in the plural and attributed to "Jasper Deane, John Deane, and Miles Whitworth," who, it was added, was "lately dead." What killed Whitworth is unknown, but it was likely an infirmity he picked up on Boon Island. Infected sores, for example, could lead to a long, painful death. He almost certainly never saw the postscript, let alone had a hand in writing it. In their postscript the Deanes declared, "Having two or three spare Pages, we think it our duty to the truth, and our selves, to obviate a barbarous and scandalous Reflection, industriously spread abroad and level'd at our ruine, by some unworthy, Malicious Persons."

Unworthy. That's the key word—ultimately the battle between the gentlemen and the seamen was being fought to determine whether or not John Deane, and to a lesser extent his brother, should be considered gentlemen, worthy of good company on the Royal Exchange, in government circles, and among London's artists and intellectuals. In eighteenth-century England these were no small stakes; only a gentleman could be rich, respected, hold political power, and circulate in all of the social circles that mattered. Members of the nobility were born into such gentility, but they were increasingly made uneasy and crowded by Englishmen who became wealthy enough in the vigorous market economy to be indistinguishable from the old landed gentry.

A gentleman was required to have money, which could buy him all of the symbols of his status such as a large city townhouse, landed estate, elegant furnishings, fancy clothing, powdered wigs, a fine coach, and a wife and friends from a similar class. Such adornments, however, did not by themselves make a gentleman. Instead they were understood as reflections of his character. A gentleman was wise, well read, enterprising, well mannered, honest, pious, patriotic, selfless, and a leader, and the symbols of status supposedly flowed from a man's gentile character. The loss of that reputation could destroy the gentleman, setting him adrift into the great sea of humanity.

Whether out of a desire for justice or revenge, "sailors" Christopher Langman, Nicholas Mellen, and George White hit John Deane where it hurt most—at his reputation as a gentleman. They charged the captain not only with criminality and negligence, but also—even more damning among the upper crust—with brutality, impiety, dishonesty, poverty, profanity, cowardice, greed, ingratitude, and a failure to lead. Actions that were indeed, as Jasper Deane writes, "level'd at our ruine."

Upon reading Deane's new version with its postscript, "only sailors" Langman, Mellan, and White took an extraordinary step. Instead of quietly walking away, as most seamen in their social and financial position probably would have done—their points made, their blows landed—they escalated the conflict. Surprisingly, they prepared to meet Captain Deane and his allies on the captain's terms, in print, a playing field usually reserved for gentlemen, not lowly commoners. The trio may have made the decision to publish their version of events on their own, but with the war of words heating up, and the Deanes' *Narrative* selling, it's quite possible that they had the encouragement of a publisher.

During this period booksellers and publishers were overlapping occupations. John Deane's *Narrative* was sold by the bookseller/publisher, Sarah Popping. Women had a long history in the stationer's trades—nuns had labored at the Ripoli Monastery Press in Florence near the advent of printing, and the first copies of the American Declaration of Independence were printed by a woman, Mary Catherine Goddard. In England in 1711, 7 percent of all printers or stationers were women, and there were probably more, as many women who may have in practice acted the part of principle printer were hidden behind their husbands' or fathers' names. Most who came to own printing or bookselling businesses did so through male family members, though 108 women entered the trade through apprenticeships between 1666 and 1800.

Popping was a tough, businsess-savvy, street-wise woman, as most female printers and booksellers had to be in order to survive. She'd later be arrested for unlawfully usurping parliamentary privilege by pirating an account of an official debate, but she soon found enough excuses to obtain a discharge. She knew how to work the system, and in the case of the unfolding *Nottingham Galley* story, she likely saw an opportunity.

One indication of the sensation caused by the handwritten depositions and the second publication of Deane's *Narrative* is the appearance of an abridged version of Captain Deane's *Narrative,* published by John Dunton titled, *A Sad and Deplorable Account of the Sufferings, Preservation and Deliverance of Capt. John Deane.* Its introduction garishly described how the castaways were "fain to Feed upon Dead Bodies, which being all consum'd; they were going to cast Lots which should next Devour'd." It has been suggested this was an unauthorized version, but the bit about "casting of Lots" printed on the cover seems to be the only significant change from the original full Jasper Deane–edited version. Dunton claimed that his edition was authorized, and there is no reason to disbelieve him; it would have made sense for the Deane brothers to flood the market in order to drown out the voices of Langman, Mellen, and White. The Dunton version of the Deane *Narrative* is nicely edited, with the narration coming from someone shipwrecked with Captain Deane, presumably his brother Jasper. The financially struggling Dunton probably printed this shorter version of the story in order to cash in on the sensation, a story, Dunton wrote, "very well known by most merchants on the *Royal Exchange.*"

Popping was probably not surprised that the Deane *Narrative* was creating quite a stir on the streets and in the coffeehouses, as reported to her by mercury traders. Her own bookstore was near the Royal Exchange, and she would have heard the reaction as gentlemen came in to buy the captain's *Narrative*. It may well be that Langman, Mellen, and White took the initiative all on their own and sought out Popping, the same publisher used by the Deane brothers, but it is also quite likely that Popping herself seized the initiative—there was obviously money to be made by fully exploiting such a sensational story. This is hinted at by the attributions at the bottom of the rival stories. Deane's *Narrative* was "printed *by* R. Tooke" and "sold *by* S. Popping," while Langman, Mellen, and White's *Account* was "printed *for* S. Popping." In the case of the sailors' *Account*, Popping appears as the publisher.

Did Popping help Langman, Mellen, and White write their *Account?* Obviously a few exceptional sailors could write competently, even forcefully. A poor seaman might, with ambition and determination, learn to write and love the written word. Months at sea gave him plenty of time and probably shipmates who could help. Perhaps Langman liked to write. His rank among the sailors and the subtly of the arguments in his depositions suggest that he was the principle author, with Mellen and White sitting at his elbows as he drafted the *Account* they all signed.

When their "*A True Account of the Voyage of the* Nottingham-Galley *of* London, John Deane Commander, from the *River* Thames *to* New England" appeared, it magnified the uproar created by the publication of John Deane's *Narrative*. People were talking about it everywhere. The dueling documents helped make the story of Boon Island the most famous tale of mutiny and shipwreck of the eighteenth century—that is, until a crew of sailors rebelled on a ship called HMS *Bounty* in 1789.

Chapter 16

THE GROWING PUBLIC INTEREST IN THE STORY OF THE *NOTTINGHAM Galley* meant that Christopher Langman, Nicholas Mellen, and George White stood a good chance of earning back the sum they'd put into making their depositions and might even turn a small profit. Their *Account* sold for six pence—twice as much as the Captain's—and it was a fine complement to the *Narrative*. Captain John Deane's story alone was plenty compelling, but read with Langman, Mellen, and White's rebuttal, the tale achieved a whole new level of intrigue. Together, the contrasting perspectives had the capacity to generate many hours of debate and chatter in the coffeehouses of London. And conveniently for Langman, Mellen, and White, and also publisher Sarah Popping, the publication of Deane's *Narrative* primed the London market nicely for their more expensive *Account*.

Sinking their teeth into the captain's *Narrative*, Langman, Mellen, and White held back nothing. They took Deane apart, passage by passage, pointing out even the smallest disagreements.

Their most potent argument came in response to a passage in Jasper Deane's introduction, which was written when he very wrongly assumed he could win over his opponents. First, argued Jasper Deane, there should be no question regarding the veracity of his brother's *Narrative*, because he was a gentleman, as anyone who knew him could attest.

Jasper wrote, "And for the Satisfaction of others, I would only need offer, that both his Character and my own may be easily gain'd by Enquiry." Deane urged his readers to believe him simply because he and his brother were members of the same class of men as their reading audience—gentlemen. But then he went on to write a fatal sentence, and it was here that the Deane brothers paid the biggest price for assuming the cooperation of Langman, Mellen, and White and failing to revise the *Narrative* when it became clear that the uppity sailors were going to fight back. "Likewise," continued Jasper, "several of his [John Deane's] Fellow Sufferers being now in Town, their Attestations might be procur'd, if saw a real Necessity."

Naturally Langman, Mellen, and White jumped all over this. It was the first point they made in the introduction of their *Account,* referring to the claim as a "Notorious Falsehood." They had told Jasper Deane to his face that the story he wished to publish "was not true," and none of the survivors of the wreck of the *Nottingham Galley* would back the Deane brothers' *Narrative,* suggested the trio. And unlike the Deanes, they name every surviving member of the ordeal. Here again, the issue of social class comes into play. The Deanes didn't want to sully their *Narrative* with the names of unwashed sailors whose testimonies were suspect because of their low social position.

Langman, Mellen, and White focused their attack on two vulnerabilities. First, they relentlessly hammered away at John Deane's reputation as a gentleman, showing that they fully understood the rules, values, and definitions of the social order under which they lived. In so doing they gave themselves credibility by honoring that social order, even identifying themselves as "only sailors," and thus acknowledging their inferior place on its ladder. They tipped their hats to the ancient class structure, but they also deployed the more modern legal authority of sworn testimony. The trio closed out their introduction with, "And since what we deliver is upon Oath, we hope it will obtain Credit sooner than the bare Word of Captain Deane, his brother, and Mr. Whitworth, who were all three interested persons . . . Besides Mr. Whitworth is since dead, so that the Captain has no Vouchers but himself and his Brother, and how little credit they deserve, will sufficiently appear by what follows."

Indeed, in the whole of Captain Deane's *Narrative,* there were precious few "vouchers." Hardly anyone was named besides the captain. Deane offered no corroboraters. He did mention his two "honored Friends," the leading gentlemen of Portsmouth, New Hampshire, John Wentworth and

John Plaisted, but Deane was obliged to thank these men and, to refer to them as "Friends," was to use their social status and reputations to serve his own. There was also a reference to Captains Long and "Purver," or "Furber," who evacuated the castaways. These gentlemen could attest to no more than Captain Deane's behavior in Portsmouth after the rescue, and Portsmouth was a long voyage away from London. (The uncertainty over the spelling of Furber's name could have suggested to the reader that Deane and Furber had never been personally close friends, which was useful for Deane if Furber had indeed become disgusted with the captain and evicted him.)

The three sailors, in contrast, paraded a list of seemingly disinterested witnesses before the reader. First, they named all of the survivors of the wreck except the ship's boy. Then they mentioned the ships they encountered on the voyage, the *Sheerness,* whose captain and crew could have attested that the *Nottingham Galley* left the safety of the convoy, and the *Pompey,* whose Captain Den, they said, beheld the odd behavior aboard the *Nottingham Galley* off Newfoundland. For witnesses in Portsmouth, they repeatedly invoked the name of Judge Samuel Penhallow, an eminent and honorable leader in that community who Deane failed to mention. In fact, Langman, Mellen, and White seemed to have urged any persons interested in the story to inquire almost anywhere in Portsmouth, New Hampshire, to see what kind of reputation John Deane left behind. Sworn depositions and the many individuals named by Langman, Mellen and White, were damning weapons against the representations of John Deane, whose *Narrative* was weakly defended by comparison.

John and Jasper Deane were not without some persuasive arguments of their own, however. Their most powerful points appeared in the postscript to the *Narrative,* and the first and most obvious one has always dogged the case of John Deane's opponents. What sort of madman would deliberately run a ship onto a rocky shore in a violent storm? The charge sounded as "ridiculous" then, as it does today. As the captain noted: "'Twas more than Ten Thousand to one but every man had perish'd."

Sailors Mellen and White let their hatred of Captain Deane cloud their reasoning on this issue, but Langman more prudently hedged so that he never explicitly accused John Deane of deliberately driving the *Nottingham Galley* onto the Maine shore. In the depositions the distinctions Langman drew were subtle, while the brash statements of Mellen and White were not. By the time they got around to publishing their *Account,* Mellen and White wisely backed off from their insistence that Captain Deane purposefully wrecked the ship. Their new position appeared as part of the very lengthy title of their *Account,* where they stated that the ship was lost "by the Captain's obstinacy."

The Deanes moved on to address the charges of insurance fraud. In their revised *Narrative,* for the first time, the brothers acknowledged "being chas'd by two large Privateers, in their Passage North-about to Killybegs." But the only admission they made was that Whitworth and Captain Deane agreed they would run the *Nottingham Galley* aground; rather than be captured. And they challenged anyone with knowledge of them—or another investor in the ship—taking out more insurance than £250 between England and Ireland, or £300 between Ireland and New England, or collecting more than £226 17s after expenses, to "publish it by Way of Advertisement in some common News Paper and we undernam'd do hereby promise to make the utmost Satisfaction, and stand convict to be the greatest Villians in the Universe."

The postscript to the Deane *Narrative* concluded strongly:

> *And Now, let the World judge whether 'tis reasonable to imagine we shou'd willfully lose a Ship of 120 Tuns, besides a valuable Interest in Cargo in such a Place, where the Commander (as well as the Rest) must unavoidably run the utmost Hazard of perishing in the most miserable Manner, and all this to recover £226 17s how absurd and ridiculous is such a Supposition, and yet this is the Reproach we at present labor under, so far as to receive daily ignominious Scandals upon our Reputations, and injurious Affronts and Mobbings to our Faces.*

The "injurious Affronts and Mobbings" not only identified the Deanes' opponents as rabble, but also suggested that going out in London was becoming difficult for the Deane brothers. Apparently the sensation of the story was making celebrities out of the pair—and the sailor friends of Langman, Mellen, and White were making their lives miserable.

But what of their argument? It's very easy to believe that no one in their right mind would intentionally drive a ship on a rocky shore in a violent winter storm; here Langman, Mellen, and White were delinquent in adjusting their tack. And the potential reward from the insurance fraud doesn't seem proportionate to the risks involved in the scheme. Could it be that Langman, Mellen, and White were completely wrong in claiming that John Deane, Jasper Deane, and Miles Whitworth were deliberately trying to lose the ship?

Or do the pieces to this puzzle simply fit together in another way?

Chapter 17

IN THEIR INDIVIDUAL DEPOSITIONS BOATSWAIN NICHOLAS MELLEN AND Sailor George White were convinced that Captain John Deane tried to lose the *Nottingham Galley* to commit insurance fraud. If that was really the goal of Captain Deane, his brother Jasper Deane, and Miles Whitworth, they weren't very quiet about their intentions. On each of the two days they faced the French privateers, Whitworth was overheard by crew members admitting that the ship was over-insured, almost as if he wanted it widely known. What if their talk of insurance fraud was only a cover for another more serious crime, one that ordinary English sailors were less likely to go along with?

Mellen and White appear to have taken the word of the Deane brothers and Whitworth at face value, stating unequivocally that on the second encounter with the French privateers, Captain Deane intended to run the *Nottingham Galley* aground on the Irish shore. Once again Langman had a slightly different perspective on the situation than his fellow sailors. The first mate said, "The Day following they saw the Privateers again, when the said John Deane (contrary to the Will of this Deponent) would have brought the Ship *Nottingham* to an Anchor, which if done, she would in all probability have been taken."

Langman made no mention of the intent, real or otherwise, to run the ship on shore.

By the time the three disaffected seamen got around to writing their *Account,* the individual opinions had been discussed at length, shared with others, and clarified so that they could finally conclude that Captain Deane lost the ship through "obstinacy" on the night of the storm, and earlier "endeavour'd to betray her [the *Nottingham Galley*] to the French, or run her ashore." For maximum impact, they deployed their new language in the very title of their *Account*. The use of the word *betray* suggested a crime even uglier than insurance fraud—treason.

John and Jasper Deane must have well understood that many members of London society would have suspected them of trying something more sinister than insurance fraud. When they finally got around to discussing the encounter with the French privateers, the Deane brothers claimed that as a last resort, if there were no means of escape, they would, as they discussed aboard the *Nottingham Galley*, "run the Ship on Shore *and burn her*." Did they add the part about burning so that their readers would not think that they intended the French to capture the *Nottingham*'s cargo? Or as Langman vaguely suggested, could the real intention of John Deane, Jasper Deane, and Miles Whitworth have been to *sell* the *Nottingham Galley* and its cargo to the French?

Smuggling was a well-known problem. In 1704 the Queen Ann's Lord Treasurer had dispatched a special customs official, Captain Thomas Knox, to Ireland to investigate the widespread reports of smuggling activity and to take measures to suppress it. Knox and many other witnesses testified before a committee of the House of Lords that an extensive illicit wartime trade was taking place between the British Isles and France. Most of this underground commerce went through Ireland, because the Emerald Isle lacked a strong customs service and had many islands and inlets convenient for hiding and, most of all, the Irish were primarily Roman Catholic and therefore not particularly loyal to the English Crown.

Knox reported that a number of Irish merchants departed with James II at the time of the Glorious Revolution and took up shop in the western ports of France, and numerous English sea captains captured by French privateers gave evidence before the committee of the many Irish and English ships they witnessed in these French ports. It was said that a "Great trade" was "carried on with France from Dublin, Waterford, Ross, Cork and Lymrick." A Captain Fowles, who was transported as a prisoner from Martinique to France, testified, "In April last, going between Olerone and St. Martin, they met Six Sail of English and Irish Vessels, coming out among many *French* Ships; and One Ketch coming near the Ship in which Captain Fowles was on, he asked, 'Whither they were bound?' And they answering, 'For Ireland.'"

The depth of the smuggling problem is indicated by the participation of Irish officials in the trade and their close cooperation with French privateers. A Captain Edwards, held prisoner at La Rochelle, France, likewise reported:

> He saw Wm. Williamson taking an Account of Provisions then landing out of a Pink; which, Williamson told him, belonged to Alderman Bell of Dublin. He also said, There were Fifteen English and Irish Ships in the Port, who waited to go out with several Ships of War that lay in the Road, and were reported to be victualed, and some of them loaden with Provisions out of those Ships.

Captain Knox recommended a number steps be taken to suppress smuggling on the Irish coast, but evidently the scale of the problem and the cost of fixing it were too much for the English government, which was already paying for an expensive war fought in many different parts of the world. Knox quit his post, wanting no part of a hopeless and thankless job with insufficient pay, but he remained troubled by what he had found during his tour in Ireland. Four years later, in 1708, he published pamphlets about the ongoing problem, which had only gotten worse.

Another pamphleteer, who went by the initials RF and claimed to know his business very well, protested the lack of a sensible policy to thwart this extensive smuggling trade. "Though 'tis prohibited by an Act of parliament [trade with France]," wrote RF, "we find a surreptitious Trade continually carrying on thither, in contempt of the same . . . Rarely have anyone been exchequer'd though taken in the very Fact of Smuggling, unless it happens to be some senseless Rogue, with a Purse (or 'Parle' or 'Purie') as empty as his Pate, and no Friend or faithful Confident at his Back."

Smuggling was attractive for reasons other than simply financial gain—ideological interests coexisted alongside material ones in the illicit wartime trade with France. In 1710 it had been barely twenty years since the Glorious Revolution, when William of Orange, stadtholder or governor, of the Dutch Republic, invaded England at the invitation of English political forces hostile to James II, a Catholic king in the process of setting up an absolute monarchy. William secured the right of parliamentary sovereignty for the English ruling class in return for military support against his arch foe, Louis XIV of France. A significant number of English, not to mention Irish and Scots, refused to accept William as king and remained loyal to the dethroned James II, who was recognized as the rightful heir to the English throne by Louis XIV, and lived under the French king's protection.

As Knox points out, some Irish merchants loyal to James II fled with him to France to set up businesses that served both their financial interests and the man they believed was their rightful sovereign. Many other English, Irish, and Scots, especially members of the nobility and Roman Catholics, openly supported a restoration of James II's line. Known as Jacobites, they even had their own coffeehouse in London. Though trading with the enemy was considered treason, the Jacobites believed they were the loyal patriots, fighting to enthrone James III, who in terms of heredity was the rightful heir to the British Crown. English, Scottish, and Irish Jacobites would welcome James III's landing in England with an army of Frenchmen, just as those who disagreed with them had welcomed William of Orange with his army of Dutchmen in 1689. At least their Jacobite army would be lead by a legitimate English king, and not a foreign usurper.

Smuggling is a necessarily murky business. Underground traders took great pains to conceal their operations. Knox and RF only provide hints and generalities of the numerous methods of exchanging goods between the British Isles and France during the War of Spanish Succession. According to Knox, Irish products, especially wool, were disguised as barrels of beef and "conveyed into Creeks or Islands." There, "*French* privateers, upon certain signals, call for them, and take them off from those Islands, near the Shoar, where they are left for them, there being a secret correspondence, as well as *French Passes* procured for the support of the

Practice." RF wrote tellingly, "By sham Captures, what gross Cheats and Abuses are the Work of every Day, are numberless; *viz* by taking ships freighted with Wine and Brandy, by private Contract and Assignation: By Seizures being made by the Importers own Information, after private Agreement and Bonds enter'd into between him and the Seizor." In other words English ships were making "agreements" to be captured by French privateers.

Could this be what Captain Deane and his associates were up to when First Mate Langman stopped them? And could it be the reason for the great delay in Ireland?

Knox's pamphlet stresses the trade of French wine and brandy for English wool. These were the most common items exchanged. But what of the *Nottingham Galley*'s cargo of cordage? Knox noted before Parliament that the trade between the two nations was not only about wool and wine, but that "*French* Fleets, Privateers and Plantations [were] furnished with provisions by this Traffick." In fact there is every indication that the successful delivery of rope to France would have been a bonanza to the merchant who delivered it. The economy of France was utterly ruined by the war. Mother Nature hadn't been kind to France either; there were severe drought and starvation in 1709.

But one industry thrived: shipbuilding. Privateering was the engine that drove the economies of France's western ports. Much of the commerce came from neutral nations—the Dutch who openly traded with their enemy—as well as from privateers. In 1708 famous English privateer Woodes Rogers stopped a neutral Swedish vessel making for France the long way over Scotland and around the west coast of Ireland, a route usually designed to avoid encounters with English men-o-war. Some drunken sailors aboard the Swedish vessel told Rogers that there was gunpowder and cables aboard, but the search of the ship turned up nothing and it was let go. (Members of Rogers's crew, hungry for plunder, were unconvinced of the Swedish ship's innocence and had to be disciplined for mutinous behavior after the potential prize was released.)

In the French port of St. Malo there was a "persistent demand for the building of ships and houses and for the feeding of an inflated war-time population" wrote historian J. S. Bromley. The money to buy these goods came almost exclusively from privateering. But every year from 1709 to 1711 one third to one half of all of St. Malo's privateers were captured or sunk, which meant new boats had to replace them—the demand for all types of naval stores must have been tremendous in this port alone.

As an illustration of the constant and often urgent need for cordage, an English diplomat once remarked that if a certain convoy carrying hemp from Russia "should by accident Miscary, it will be impossible for His Majesty to fit out any ships of war for the next year, by which means the whole navy of England will be rendered perfectly useless." An English frigate of the period might have one quarter of its hold packed with extra cordage at the beginning of a voyage. If the English navy, with its command of the sea lanes, could come close to running out of rope and cable, then demand for cordage in the besieged French privateering ports in 1710 can easily be imagined.

The *Nottingham Galley* carried a cargo valuable—perhaps extremely valuable—in any French port. And if naval stores were in high demand for the outfitting of ships for privateering ventures, then the sale of a ship itself, like the *Nottingham Galley*, a fast, shallow-draft vessel perfect for the combined uses of privateering and smuggling, would have brought a very great profit indeed. On top of the proceeds from the sale of the vessel and its cargo, the Deane brothers and Miles Whitworth could have collected the much-discussed insurance money, the frosting on the cake. If true, these gentlemen were playing for much higher stakes than the supposed and relatively paltry insurance-fraud scheme, and if successful, the Deane family could have restored its flagging financial status in just this one bold stroke.

Other details of the story are consistent with a smuggling scenario. A fast galley might well break from a convoy to arrive in port first for the most favorable market conditions. But the *Nottingham Galley* already had its principle cargo—cordage—on board. The slightly better price it might get on cheese by arriving in port first seems small compared to the risk of traveling alone in waters known to be rife with privateers.

Also striking is the destination in Ireland to which the *Nottingham Galley* sailed, Killybegs, Donegal County, in the north. This region tends to be rough and rocky, fine for the raising of sheep, but not the best dairy country. For milk products, a ship normally would have called on one of Ireland's southwestern ports, especially Cork. The Irish had become great consumers of dairy products, and milk had become an unusually popular beverage. Donegal County produced enough milk for local markets, but southwest Ireland was by far the best place to look for low-priced dairy goods suitable for export. Convoys were very regular to the southern coast of Ireland, and in that area English merchant shipping had the added protection of five to eight English warships, which were on permanent station to deter an invasion of Ireland and prosecute smuggling. Captain Deane, however, ordered the *Nottingham Galley* to northern Ireland, where there was virtually no chance of encountering an English warship, and where buying cheese to sell in Boston, or anywhere else, would be much more difficult.

If the Deanes and Whitworth were indeed set on smuggling, the greatest obstacle to their success was aboard their own ship: sailors who were likely to rebel against trading with the enemy. Often resentful of the English class system—or at least disdainful of officers and gentlemen who failed to live up to the expectations embodied in their titles and positions—common English sailors were plenty patriotic. In the voluminous journal of English seafaring life written by Edward Barlow, one of the finest windows into the life of British sailors of the period, there is never indication of the men being anything less than zealously devoted to king (or queen) and country. Insurance fraud was one thing. If a particular set of English gentlemen were intent on deceiving another set, it probably mattered little to a common sailor, so long as he got paid. Any hint of treason, however, and the sailors would almost certainly have resisted. Perhaps this duplicity is what Langman suspected all along.

The encounter with the French privateers—and the subsequent events laid out by Langman, Mellen, and White—are consistent with the methods used in smuggling as described by Knox and the pamphleteer

RF; particularly the latter's reference to "sham captures." The meeting of the *Nottingham Galley* and the French privateers could well have been a rendezvous planned after the signing of a contract—or perhaps one of the Deanes or Whitworth carried a French pass, identifying them as lawful traders rather than prizes of war. The ships met near a remote shore and an island of the sort used by smugglers. Even if Langman's hint that the Deane brothers never intended to run the *Nottingham Galley* aground is wrong, a large and well-equipped French landing party would have had no opposition on shore and could easily have seized the cargo. The Deanes may have felt it necessary in their rebuttal to add in the part about burning the grounded ship and cargo should it have come to that.

Neither the Deane brothers nor Langman and his allies ever explained anywhere exactly what Whitworth was doing aboard the *Nottingham Galley.* Jasper Deane's presence might be justified because the ship was seven eighths his, and he owned a significant share of the cargo, which made it entirely reasonable that he should act as "supercargo." But Jasper Deane says nothing about a similar stake owned by Whitworth. Assuming that what Langman, Mellen, and White heard was correct, Whitworth stood to collect a small percentage of the £200 in insurance money. For a man with an estate worth upward of £2,000, it would have been a high-risk game in terms of his own reputation and personal safety for a comparatively modest return.

What was he doing on this voyage then?

Gentlemen didn't take late-season pleasure cruises across the Atlantic in 1710. In a smuggling scenario, Whitworth stood to make a sum of money more in keeping with the risks he took. He could have been a French-speaking representative of a number of other investors in on the scheme, an active and zealous Jacobite, or he might have had contacts in France. Nothing is certain, except that Whitworth must have sailed on the *Nottingham Galley* for some reason—and nothing in Captain Deane's story accounts for it.

The theory that the *Nottingham Galley* sailed for Northern Ireland to rendezvous with French privateers and avoid English warships—and not to buy cheese at Killybegs—is also supported by her very long stay in port. It's not unreasonable to assume that they were stuck in Killy-begs for forty-two days because they couldn't find a cargo fit for Boston, France, or both, in such a remote corner. Also, if they had missed a rendezvous with French privateers, there would have been time to plan another meeting, or possibly acquire a French pass that would work in Canadian waters. If a ship sailed ahead to give word of a new rendez-vous off Cape Sable, the recent taking of Port Royal by the English could have disrupted the plan.

When the *Nottingham Galley* found another ship off Newfoundland, the Deanes and Whitworth are said to have assumed it was French, put on their fine clothes, and plied their crew with alcohol. Yes, wearing their fine clothes might have kept them from being stolen if they were cap-tured, but the scene painted by Langman, Mellen, and White is one of the three gentlemen anticipating a happy meeting of friends or partners. John Deane, Jasper Deane, and Miles Whitworth could easily have been Jacobites, or have had Jacobite sympathies. Later events suggest, however, that if Captain Deane was a Jacobite, his convictions didn't run deep. But, then, John Deane always put his own interests first.

Jacobite leanings among the investors in the *Nottingham Galley* voy-age may help explain one of the oddest discrepancies between the accounts written by Captain Deane and his opponents. In Deane's *Narrative* there is only one hero, not counting Deane himself, and that is the character of the "Swede," the intrepid foreigner who builds a raft out of the thin-nest stock of materials under conditions of great physical disability, then insists on personally attempting the perilous paddle to the mainland.

The man's heroic character is never questioned by Langman, Mellen, and White, but in their version he is not a Swede, but instead a "stout Dutchman." It seems almost impossible that Deane, Langman, Mellen, or White could fail to know the nationality of the one foreigner in their midst after spending months together in the close confines of the ship and then weeks together practically sleeping on top of each other.

So why lie about the Swede's—or "Dutchman's"—origins?

Because the Dutch were hated by the Jacobites for toppling their king? For their Calvinist religion, and the long wars with France into which a Dutch king had dragged England? Deane might not want the one hero in his story to be Dutch, a nationality he may have detested, or he might not have wanted it known to any Jacobite investor that he had a Dutchman aboard. Or maybe Deane changed the one foreigner aboard the *Nottingham Galley* from Dutch to Swedish because Holland was becoming generally and politically unpopular in England. Perhaps Deane didn't want to appear pro-Dutch for the purposes of marketing himself or his story.

If the Deane brothers and Whitworth were indeed attempting to engage in illicit trade with the French, then they were guilty of treason, which by its nature is a very serious crime. The cordage that reached French ports could be used to help outfit French privateers who might in turn raid English commerce and even kill English sailors. Treason though it was, it was in its mildest form. Context is important. The French were probably going to obtain the supplies they needed anyway; it was a matter of who would supply them, at what profit, and in what time frame. Neutral ships carried all manner of goods into French ports. England's Dutch allies traded with France throughout the war, and at times that commerce included naval stores.

As Thomas Knox and the pamphleteer RF suggest, trade from the British Isles to France was so rampant that it seemed to discriminate against honest merchants. And to a significant segment of the English ruling class, the war with France had always been a mistake. To an even greater number of gentlemen, including the Tory faction that by 1710 controlled the government, peace and legal trade with France was just around the corner. The Court of Louis XIV was already moving to exploit the rift between the English and Dutch allies by offering trading passes to English merchants who had formerly gone to Dutch traders. The Deane brothers and Whitworth could have thought of themselves, not as traitors, but as enterprising merchants simply seizing an opportunity. Anyone found trading with the French in 1710 would be publically scorned in most social circles—a devastating consequence for would-be gentlemen—but with time they would not be beyond redemption.

Whether or not the Deane brothers and Miles Whitworth were in fact actively attempting to smuggle their cargo is somewhat of a moot point in the court of public opinion, however, because actually guilty or not, their actions as reported by Langman, Mellen, and White made them look guilty.

When war broke out between his brother and their implacable crew members, John Deane may have been away from London paying his last respects to his friend Whitworth in Burton Lazars. And perhaps he would have heard about what became of the Whitworth estate. The reading of Whitworth's will raises more intriguing questions and answers few. But it does corroborate what Boatswain Mellen insists he heard on that fateful afternoon. The document suggests that Whitworth did indeed take out a £200 insurance policy on a one-eighth share in the *Nottingham Galley*, which was purchased from Jasper Deane.

A very wealthy gentleman troubling himself to buy a one-eighth stake in a small ship is a curious thing, but it may have enabled him to hold a title to the vessel and then buy extra insurance. The £200 insurance payout was supposed to be left to Mile's son, Charles, who, as it turns out, entered the stage to play another important role in the final act of the *Nottingham Galley* story.

A very mysterious turn.

Charles Whitworth occupies a peculiar place in the will. The beginning of Miles Whitworth's last testament, drawn up in 1708, lists seven heirs, including his wife Katherine, their three sons, and their three daughters. Each of the sons was to receive an inheritance of £400, but Charles's name is curiously absent. It first appears in an amendment to the will drawn up almost on the eve of the voyage in March 1710. That is when Charles Whitworth alone is given the one-eighth stake in the *Nottingham Galley* plus £200 should his father pass away. If the one-eighth part was insured for £200, then that brought his total inheritance to the same £400 sum as his brothers.

But why does Charles appear in the will as an afterthought? Usually another child is added to a will if they are born after the initial drafting, so maybe Charles entered the picture sometime after 1708. Or perhaps he was born earlier, estranged from his father, or illegitimate, and only reconciled by 1710.

The Whitworths were more forgiving—as we shall see—than the captain's own brother. The Whitworths never blamed John Deane for the wreck. Charles, far from holding John Deane responsible for the death of his father, forgave and absolved him completely. Their relationship would serve as powerful testimony to Deane's ability to convince others of his good intentions and conduct. And in the whole story of the *Nottingham Galley* affair, Charles Whitworth—a man who never sailed with Deane or spent time on the island with him—serves as John Deane's most powerful character witness.

Back in London the battle for public opinion was being lost by the Deane brothers. John Deane may have made his amends with the Whitworth family, but to his horror his name and reputation in the city were sinking faster than did his ship. Three seamen—a first mate, a boatswain, and a common sailor—who seemed to have had nothing to gain for themselves, had gone to the trouble to pay for legal depositions, and most extraordinarily, to write and publish their *Account* of the voyage, questioning their captain's credibility as a gentleman and his loyalty to Queen Anne.

In the conclusion to their story, Langman, Mellen, and White declare, "All this we Avouch to be Truth and have no other End in publishing it, but to testify our Thankfulness to God for his Great Deliverance, and to give others Warning not to trust their Lives or Estates in the hands of so wicked and brutish a Man [as Captain John Deane]."

The words of the three sailors came off as simple, earnest, and Christian, and the public at large seemed inclined to believe them. Their story, while overstating matters in places, was too involved and nuanced to be a fabrication. What they didn't say regarding the possibility of smuggling probably came off more powerfully through implication than it would have had the sailors made the charge directly. Common sailors may have lacked a full understanding of the burgeoning illicit trade with France, or the sophisticated ways of corrupt merchants, but the gentlemen traders of London knew full well what a range of complicated games were being played by unscrupulous smugglers and Jacobite collaborators.

Captain Deane looked to all the world like a liar, a criminal, a coward,
and perhaps even a traitor to the crown. He was an admitted cannibal.
And many of his peers in London considered him as no gentleman worthy of good company. He and his brother would have to leave town.

Of course, the story didn't have to end this way. The enmity the men
had for the captain was his own creation.

Chapter 18

It happened off the coast of Cape Porpoise, province of Maine. The single moment when everything turned, when anger and resentment burned into pure hate. In the wintery fog that bitter morning, one thing became clear to Captain John Deane—he had to be wary of his first mate. Here was Christopher Langman again openly contradicting him in front of the crew, telling everyone the captain didn't even know where they made landfall. Langman was still ready to rebel if he felt he had cause to do so. Apparently making an example of a number of the sailors during the crossing hadn't been enough. Langman found Captain Deane contemptible, and Deane knew it. Nothing could be done about that, but it was infuriating. Langman could think what he pleased, but he had to be taught to keep his opinions to himself and not infect the crew. New measures were necessary to secure the first mate's obedience, and Deane resolved to act.

A short while after their argument, though, Captain Deane took a different tack, announcing the end of water rationing, often customary upon the first sight of land. The storm was already beginning to toss the ship, but the captain seemed to believe a bit of celebration was in order. He gathered the crew on deck with appropriate ceremony and went below himself to get the water "to serve" the men.

First Mate Langman already had a bottle in his hand and waited for the return of Deane. He was probably curious what the Deane brothers were up to now. As he stood there, Jasper Deane walked over and took the bottle from him. The captain's brother faced Langman, raised the bottle, and "struck him" with it, surprising him with the blow. The strike was powerful, and the first mate was dazed.

Seconds later the captain reappeared up out of the hold. But rather than water for the men, he had a club in his hand, a "Periwig Block," a wooden stand "such as Barbers make Wigs on." Approaching Langman from behind, the captain swung the block quickly up over his head and repeatedly brought it down with force on the crown of the first mate, striking him "three blows on the Head." Already reeling from Jasper's strike, the first mate collapsed, hitting the deck hard. "We all thought that he had kill'd him," remembered Boatswain Nicholas Mellen and Seaman George White, "for he lay dead some time, and lost a great deal of Blood."

No captain, whether commanding a powerful man-o-war or pirate ship, could tolerate dissent, especially from his first mate, and the Deanes stood over Langman, offering him as an example. Of course the Deanes could have put everything behind them after Captain Deane and First Mate Langman had their disagreement, sailing on to Boston to simply sell their cargo, but to back down at that point would have flown in the face of all cultural expectations aboard ship. It would have shamed Deane in front of his brother and Miles Whitworth and would have made him look weak in front of the crew. Here he was in the same situation he found himself in after leaving Killybegs. So again he struck, and he struck brutally.

Langman lay there on the deck bleeding out—it was a severe beating—but in the annals of the sea, such a thrashing was certainly not unheard of. A sailor named Gilbert Lamb returned late to his ship to receive several blows to his head from a piece of oak at the hand of his captain. The concussion he received rendered him unable to "swallow any victuals" except what was spoon-fed to him by his comrades. In 1707 a Captain Wherry put his thumb into a sailor's eye socket and hammered it in with his free hand and "in that manner willfully, designedly, & malitiously maimed & put out" his eye.

Even the choice of implement—a wigmaker's stand—to administer the discipline wasn't all that surprising. Sea captains of the period often chose exotic instruments with which to beat down their disobedient sailors. In addition to the usual sticks and canes, sailors report to have received blows to the head with a stone mug, a bull's foot, a "Manyrocker (which is a tough Root as thick as a Man's Legg)," and even "an Elephant's dry'd Pizle." There was a nice symbolism to the periwig's block—the place where a gentleman kept his wig for polite company, it was both effete and upper crust. It's so apropos that there's a temptation to question it in the account of Deane's opponents. But Captain Deane himself refers to fleeing the sinking *Nottingham Galley* with neither "wig nor cap."

The case made by Langman, Mellen, and White against Captain Deane contrasts with instances in which sea captains are clearly sadistic, like Howes Norris, captain of a Martha's Vineyard whaler, who in the nineteenth century worked and beat his African-American steward to death over the course of many weeks, seemingly for the pleasure of it. If the trio of deponents wanted to level false charges, they most likely would have come up with something more despicable. But it seems Deane was driven by a different set of professional, cultural, and psychological pressures.

Langman, Mellen, and White don't say how long the first mate lay on the deck bleeding as the clouds darkened around them, but they do say the sight of him was "very discouraging to the Seamen, who durst not speak to him for fear of the like treatment." Neither do they say whether he had help getting up, but most likely he was escorted below. Langman apparently stayed in his cabin nursing a traumatic brain injury for the rest of the morning and throughout the afternoon. As he lay in his bunk, his head throbbing, he must have felt the roll of the ship getting heavier and heard the wind quickening outside.

The storm was organizing into a furious nor'easter. By nightfall Boatswain Mellen, who had the watch, claims he had become alarmed by both the ferocity of the conditions and the proximity of the main. Because of the overcast skies, they'd had difficulty accurately gauging their position, and many aboard "Perceiv'd the ship in Danger by being so near land."

The boatswain sent someone below to get both Captain Deane and First Mate Langman. Of course this was like calling for matches and powder. Deane arrived on deck first, followed by Langman, who hadn't yet cleaned up from the morning's beating. "Scarce recovered," remembered Mellen, the first mate was still covered in his own blood, "all in Gore."

Langman said he told Deane that "he had no Business so near Land, except he had a Mind to lose the Ship, and therefore desir'd him to hawl further off, or else he would be ashore that Night." At this Deane flew into a rage. He told Langman "he wou'd not take his Advice though the Ship should go to the Bottom."

It was a telling remark. Deane seemed more concerned about his authority as commander of the ship than of the safety of the vessel and his men, his reason clouded by anger at his first mate and the rest of the disloyal crew. For all anyone knows, Captain Deane might have been about to change course when Langman came up on deck to again challenge his authority. In the third version of his *Narrative,* Deane said that he planned to take in sail at 10:00 p.m. Had he a good working relationship with his first mate, the captain might well have heeded his advice and dropped sail earlier or directed the vessel farther out to sea. Langman's vehement advocacy for a change in course made just such a change that much less likely. Again Deane didn't want to be seen to back down. Instead of following the mate's wiser tack, the captain pulled out a pistol and "threatened to shoot the Mate." Pointing the weapon at Langman, Deane told him he could do as he pleased, so long as it was in the confinement of his cabin.

The captain set the course for the ship—first mate be damned. In only one place in the three versions of his *Narrative* does Deane directly contradict himself, and it's here that he vacillates. In the first version of his *Narrative,* the captain reports the ship heading "something southerly." In the second version he has the ship "haling Southerly for the Massachusetts-Bay, under a hard gale of Wind at North-East." By the time Deane got around to revising his narrative in 1726, sixteen years after the fact, he changed his story, saying since "the Wind being N.E. and the Land lying N.E and S.W, they concluded it both Safe and Advisable to steer *S.W.* 'till 10 a Clock at Night and then lie by 'till Morning, with the Head of their Vessel off from Land." At this point they would have dropped a sea anchor and waited out the storm, the safest course of action.

The decision here was the fateful one. If the *Nottingham Galley* was to continue sailing virtually anywhere in the Gulf of Maine, a southerly course would have been the most prudent—moving in a straight line to the south would have placed the ship increasingly to the east of the rocky coast. Any westward course posed risks, because the wind was also driving the vessel to the southwest and there was danger in undercompensating. Then there was also the issue of Captain Deane having no idea where he and his little ship actually were. Sailing blind and disoriented, caution should have been the rule, and he should have pushed out to sea.

But that was the course suggested by the first mate.

The stories told by the captain and the accounts of his rebellious crew began to intersect as the *Nottingham Galley* drew ever nearer to the ledges of Boon Island. One thing they agree on was that First Mate Langman was recuperating from his injury—Deane referred to him as "indisposed"; the trio referred to him as "still in his cabbin, and hardly done bleeding"—and was unable to perform his duty. And Langman, Mellen, and White said that despite the intensity of the storm that tossed the ship, the captain wasn't on deck either. "For he was then undressing himself to go to Bed, according to his usual Custom."

This left the cold and tired Boatswain Mellen at the helm and in charge on deck, overseeing consecutive watches. The ship sailed on the course of the captain's choosing—Mellen probably didn't dare stray from it, though he worried for their safety. Overhead the skies were choked with gloom: "It blew hard, accompanied with Rain and Snow," as Deane recalled. Below, the seas were sickening in their surging power—"a fury" in the Captain's words. It was Mellen who was trying to peer through the murk ahead.

And then it happened, just as they feared.

According to Mellen, without any warning, sometime "between 8 and 9 a Clock," the ship made its violent meeting with the shore, tossing the boatswain from his feet and setting the *Nottingham Galley* heeling to one side as the waves began washing over her deck.

After the ship hit ledge, the first thing Mellen did was head below to find Captain Deane. At the sight of his captain, the boatswain could no longer contain himself. For a moment, anyway, rage took the place of fear. Mellen screamed at Deane, charging that "he had made his Words good, and lost the Ship on purpose." He said that he rebuked the captain for not listening to the mate, because if he had, they would have been safe in Boston. While Langman never came out and accused Captain Deane with deliberately wrecking the ship on the night of the storm, Mellen showed no such reticence. He wanted it known that he believed Deane willfully destroyed the *Nottingham Galley* on the rocks of Maine.

Deane turned and addressed the boatswain. "The Captain bid him [Mellen] to hold his Peace. He was sorry for what had happen'd, but we must now all prepare for Death, there being no Probability to escape it." He appeared ready to give up and let the sea do what it would. Langman, Mellen, and Deane all said that some of the crewmen decided to try to survive anyway. Two went up on deck, but could not stay there because "the Sea broke all over the Ship," as it increasingly listed to one side. Mellen and another man went down into the hold to see if the hull had been breached and they were taking on water—it had and they were. The *Nottingham Galley* was both heeling badly and filling up with cold sea. The cabin, severely tilting with the ship, was a small pocket of shelter that could burst open or begin flooding from below at any moment. Deane, "who had been Cursing and Swearing before," said Langman, Mellen and White, "began to cry and howl for fear losing his Life."

Though Langman may not have believed it was Deane's intent to run the ship aground, he nevertheless held him responsible for it, and for all of the terrible suffering the victims of the wreck would endure on Boon Island thereafter. And here the Captain sat looking pathetic. "We see what brave Commanders we have nowadays, that can swagger, and curse and swear, damn and damn with their great periwigs and swords huffing and puffing," wrote a sailor of the time, "but let them face real danger and their debauchery and conscience fly in their face and they are more like 'hens before the kiat' than men." Written eight years before the wreck, the passage sounds—right down to the periwigs—as if it had come out of the mouths of Langman, Mellen, and White.

Deane, in his *Narrative*, suggested his own conduct at that critical moment was calm and collected, especially compared to members of his crew, who all but collapsed. But in the account of the three sailors, Captain

Deane panics, becoming hysterical. In a crisis 10 to 15 percent of all people experience a high degree of such behavior, including "uncontrolled weeping, confusion, screaming, and paralyzing anxiety." Cases of panic are more prevalent when the subject appears to be facing a quick death, which was certainly true as the *Nottingham Galley* bent over under the weight of the sea and took on water. A person in a state of panic becomes selfish, all sense of altruism vanishes, and behavior becomes highly irrational and illogical. It's a very human response to disaster, and it's impossible to know who will be afflicted with it until a crisis arises. According to Langmen, Mellen, and White, Deane was completely unprepared for the crisis he now faced.

After the sailors returned from inspecting the deck and the hold, the entire ship's company gathered for prayer in the main cabin, a fact mentioned in both the trio's *Account* and Captain Deane's *Narrative*. The majority seemed content to remain there for the lack of any alternative and prayed "in hopes the Ship would lie whole until till Daylight." Abandoning ship isn't always the best option in a disaster at sea. In the case of the French frigate *Medusa*, which had run aground on a sandbar, most of the ship's company fled on boats and an open raft to endure a most hellish survival experience, while the ship they left behind held together with plenty of provisions aboard for many weeks. But the *Nottingham Galley* had run aground on rocks, not a sandbar.

At this crucial point, with the fate of everyone aboard at stake, it was Langman who took action, according to Captain Deane's opponents. After some praying, "the Mate, though hardly able, went with some others above Deck, for his Surprize made him forget his Pain." Carried by adrenalin, Langman scouted the scene and then returned below and proposed cutting away the masts. Captain Deane just sat there, insisting "it was impossible for us to save our Lives." To this Langman responded angrily that it was the captain's "business to encourage the Men, and not dishearten them." The three deponents, said the captain, "cryed heartily, and begg'd the Mate to do what he could to save us, for he himself could do nothing."

A party of volunteers fell in behind Langman, climbing up on the treacherous, tilting deck, awash in pounding waves. They felled "the

Main-Mast and Foremast, which by God's Assistance prov'd the Means of our Preservation, for the Fore-Mast fell on the Rock with one End ..."

While Langman and two others worked on deck, Captain Deane, according to his critics, remained all but paralyzed. He came "upon the Deck but once when he held by the Long Boat, cryed out, and presently went down again, which greatly discouraged us." When it was evident that the foremast had landed on a rock, Langman and his team returned below to urge Captain Deane to abandon the ship via the mast. By this time the water was coming up out of the hold, and the waves and listing of the vessel made it impossible to stand on deck. Again Deane hesitated, according to Langman, and may have given thought to retrieving some items, particularly his great coat, but Langman argued "it was not time to think of saving any thing, but to get ashore as light as we cou'd." The captain never went back for his coat or money or brandy, as he claimed, but simply followed the direction of the mate. Langman eventually persuaded the captain and the remainder of the ship's company to attempt an escape by crawling out on the mast.

Langman had climbed out on the Boltsprint and had spied land, but as for shimmying out on the mast "he desir'd the Captain and the rest to go ashore before he attempted it himself." Langman couldn't swim, and his head injury likely had made him dizzy. In effect the mate would be taking the traditional role of the captain, last to abandon ship. But Captain Deane wouldn't do it. He refused to lead.

According to Langman, Mellen, and White, it was Langman who again stepped forward. "The Mate got first on the Mast and with great Difficulty escap'd to the Rock." A couple of others followed, but they apparently did not include White or Mellen. The three describe how it was nearly impossible to stand on the ledge, but Langman nevertheless "hallow'd to us to follow them, and we not hearing them any more than once, were afraid they were wash'd off by the Waves." The unknown fate of Langman and the other two men put the remainder of the ship's company into a "mighty consternation, so that we knew not whether it was best to follow them or to stay on Board until it was Day."

Below in the cabin, the remainder of the men argued and prayed once more. Captain Deane, they said, wanted to wait until morning before abandoning ship. But the sea forced the issue. Water began pouring into the main cabin where they stood, an event similar to the one Deane described, except that Deane placed himself alone in his own cabin when the water began rushing in.

The men scurried back onto the deck of the now rapidly sinking *Nottingham Galley* and in groups made their way uneasily out onto the treacherous mast "being forced to crawl upon our Hands and Knees, we were so heavy with water, and the Rock so slippery."

As the storm swirled around them—and as their ship sank into the abyss—they hauled themselves across the mast to their fates.

Epilogue

WITH THEIR REPUTATIONS SINKING FASTER THAN SCUTTLED SHIPS, John and Jasper Deane fled from London. Jasper Deane returned to their hometown of Wilford to live a life of quiet husbandry. Tenacious, restless, and ever calculating, Captain John Deane was only just beginning his adventures in the world. He put as much distance as he could between himself and his past, leaving the British Isles far behind. When history found him next he was once again at the command of a ship—in the Russian Navy of Peter the Great.

John Deane's eleven years in Russia are shrouded in even more mystery than the rest of his life, but there was one particular episode that would go down in the annals. And it was disturbingly like a certain trip he made across the North Atlantic four years prior. In 1714 Deane was ordered to relocate the fifty-two-gun man-of-war *Egudel* from Archangel to the Baltic. Once again winter was coming on and Deane was helming a vessel through treacherous waters. Deane later recorded that the ship, "after careening and repairing, sailed from Archangel, and passing the North Cape [of Norway] the last of November, with much ado got in and wintered about 25 leagues from Trondhjem, losing much of her crew through the asperity of this cold season."

Personal history repeated itself. This time, half the men in his command died.

In Russia, though, the reaction was different than it was in England. The following year, Deane was actually promoted, to the rank of Captain, and given command of the thirty-two-gun frigate *Sampson*. After his calamitous debut, Deane's fortunes took a bit of a turn, and he seems to have mastered the workings of the Russian Navy, all the while teaching himself to speak and read Russian. He became a skilled privateer for the czar, capturing twenty prizes and in so doing winning the patronage of Admiral Apraxin, the head of the Russian Admiralty. Deane's personality and values, which featured subtlety, calculation, and personal loyalty, would seem a good fit for Russian politics, but once again, Deane was undone by a controversial encounter at sea.

Captain Deane came into the Russian Navy as Peter the Great was rebuilding his fleet and recruiting foreign officers to fight his nemesis, the militant Charles XII of Sweden. In 1717, while in the Gulf of Danzig, Captain Deane's *Sampson* took two Swedish merchant ships as prizes. Just as the *Sampson*'s crews were boarding to take over the captured vessel, two ships appeared, one English, one Dutch. Until recently Britain had been on the side of Russia, but the country's adventures in Germany had prompted the English Hanoverian King George to switch sides. And now Deane found himself facing the cannons of his countrymen.

Against such odds the *Sampson* was hopelessly out gunned. Much like he had in the incident with the French privateers he encountered off Ireland, Deane chose neither to fight nor flee. The English vessel drew alongside the *Sampson,* and Deane was called aboard. According to Deane he was forced to give up his two prizes, and that's the way the matter remained for two whole years. Captain Deane was again promoted and given more responsibility.

Then things turned ugly. It didn't seem to matter how far Deane fled, his past followed him. A junior Russian officer accused Deane of taking a bribe from the English captain in exchange for the two Swedish vessels, and the charge stuck. Deane was court-martialed and found guilty, even though eleven officers and members of the crew of the *Sampson* testified in his defense. To make matters worse, the czar reduced Deane's rank to lieutenant and exiled him to the remote region of Kazan to command a barge on the Volga River. It was yet another terrible blow to Deane's reputation.

Deane received a reprieve a year later when Czar Peter, celebrating his victory over Sweden, gave a general amnesty to all disgraced foreign officers. Admiral Apraxin, who remained loyal to Deane, sent him on his way in 1722 with a letter that again referred to Deane as a "captain," a de facto restoration of his rank.

With the wreck of the *Nottingham Galley* now eleven years behind him, and his trial in Russia largely unknown, John Deane had something of a clean slate, but even after years of effective service in the Russian Navy, he had little to show for it.

Returning home Deane tried his hand at letters again. He sought to capitalize on his long experience in Russia by producing a document, "A History of the Russian Fleet during the Reign of Peter the Great," which he hoped would be useful to the English Crown. The manuscript impressively chronicled—at great length, clarity, and detail—the rise of the Russian Navy in the Baltic Sea, and it showcased Deane's keen abilities as an analyst and writer. He concluded the report by laying it "before your Majesty," signing, "Your Majesty's Most Sincerely Devoted Subject and Servant, John Deanee."

The second part of Deane's two-pronged strategy of self-promotion was the republication of the *Narrative,* the same one edited by his brother, minus the introduction and postscript. Fourteen years later Captain Deane had the field to himself; no disgruntled sailors waited in the wings to ambush him and no one questioned his characterization of himself as a man of character, brave and resourceful under circumstances of unimaginable hardship. This time Deane got what he wanted, and he saw his profile rise in the ranks of English society.

When the manuscript about the Russian Navy arrived in the hands of those in government who could help Deane, they would already be favorably acquainted with him based on his shipwreck story. In addition to being a man of character, the Russian report showed Deane to be a man of intellect, useful knowledge, and connections.

The strategy worked beyond any reasonable expectation, attracting the attention of none other than Lord Townsend, the Queen's secretary of state for the northern department, and Townsend's deputy, George Tilson. Tilson interviewed Deane and wrote to his boss, "Captain Deanee undertook to be useful to us and showed us a letter from Admiral Apraksin, who seems to be a power in that country [Russia], which persuaded us he might render service." Deane found himself appointed commercial consul at St. Petersburg, a big jump from the frigid squalor of Boon Island and his exile on a Volga barge. The post was only "colour," wrote Tilson, "but his true business is to transmit hither what intelligence he may be able to get for His Majesty's service." Deane, who proved gifted at deception, was hired by the English Crown as a spy. And he'd bring back intelligence about his friends the Russians.

Lord Townsend was primarily interested in a particular type of information. Along with many others in English government and society, he and his deputy were obsessed with the threat of a Jacobite conspiracy set on toppling the Hanoverian succession and restoring the Catholic and Absolutist Stuart monarchy to the throne of England. Most powerful and persistent conspiracy theories contain some elements of truth, and in this case there were no fewer than five actual or aborted foreign-aided Jacobite rebellions between 1689 and 1744. Plenty of Jacobites still resided in the British Isles and continued to live unhappily under a king, George I of Hanover, who they believed had no rightful claim to the English throne. Lord Townsend, who lacked reliable ears in St. Petersburg, wanted to know what role Russia might play in the ongoing drama.

With his ability to speak Russian and his background in Russian affairs, Deane was an intriguing choice for the mission. But there were still those lingering suspicions that he'd tried to trade with the French during the war, which would have made him a suspected Jacobite himself. Was Deane a Jacobite turncoat? (The very fact that he was willing to play spy on the Russians suggests he had duplicity in him.) If he was in fact loyal to George I, then that public perception that he might be disloyal made him the perfect man to penetrate any existing ring of Jacobites located in Russia.

Informing English diplomat Stephen Poyntz of Deane's mission, Townsend prefaced his note cryptically, saying, "You know John Deane as well as I do, I take him to be an honest man." If so, why did he need to say so aloud? The statement clearly suggests doubt in the halls of power.

Lord Townsend understood well enough how John Deane worked— he was supremely loyal to those above and below him who served his interests. If the posting in St. Petersburg was only about Jacobite intrigue and knowledge of Russian affairs, Deane's appointment would have gone off swimmingly. However, there was Deane's unfortunate conviction in Russia for taking the bribe and his subsequent exile to the Volga. The English merchant community in St. Petersburg tried to warn Townsend about this, but he was convinced that most of them were Jacobite traitors. Sir Nathanial Gould, on behalf of the English Russian Company, had urged against sending Deane because he was "very prejudicial to our mercantile affairs," and "very obnoxious" to the Russian government. Townsend wouldn't hear any of this, and Deane arrived at his post at St. Petersburg in the spring of 1725, only to have his credentials denied. He was forced to leave Russian soil within sixteen days.

On his way home Deane wrote a letter to Townsend's deputy, Tilson, that was vintage John Deane. (Much of the captain's correspondence over the years would carry the same themes.) His first instinct was always to plead his own innocence and then find enemies to blame for his misfortunes. Deane reminded Tilson that he'd only accepted the mission to Russia "with great reluctance, having formerly experienced the malice of that sett of men, but it was impossible for any person not present to believe with what bitterness they had persecuted me in Russia."

The captain could have turned down the post, he wrote, but he didn't want his superiors to think he was "afraid to go." His enemies in Russia, the "Jacobites" who had united with "Hollsteeners" (a reference to German enemies of King George's Hanover), were "two [*sic*] powerful for a person so much suspected as I was." Most worrisome of all to Deane were his "Implacable Enemies" at home, who "could by no means ommit so favorable an opportunity as my absence gave them, to seek my ruin" and "be rendered odious to the government whose cause I serve and by such persons as are no more friends to the government than they are to me."

Deane now had opponents far more powerful than the common sailors who had sought to sabotage him after the *Nottingham Galley* disaster, and their opinions of him, it appears, were colored by Christopher Langman's *Account*. Wherever he was, the first mate would no doubt be tickled. The ordeal of Boon Island—and the grisly things that occurred there—still loomed in Deane's background. "I make no doubt," Deane stated, "but my adversary has found means . . . of Representing me a Monster in Nature."

Deane was once again all out of luck. His Russian mission a total failure, he returned home and tried to save himself with his pen. He produced two new intelligence reports on Russia, one about the political situation since the death of Peter the Great, and the other a look at the workings of the Russian Navy. But he had been sent to Russia to flush out Jacobite conspiracy and had nothing to show for it.

Ever calculating, Deane had secured a meeting with a Jacobite courier, a young Irish military officer named Edmund O'Connor, before he left St. Petersburg, hoping something productive would come out of their networking. And in a short time something did.

With the offer of a bribe and a king's pardon, Deane apparently convinced O'Connor to betray the Jacobite cause. The captain was then able to penetrate the Jacobite ring led by the notorious agent John Archdeacon and detect an enormous conspiracy hatched against England, her liberties, and Protestantism itself. It seemed that Spain, Russia, and Austria planned an attack in six months' time, with one army landing in Scotland and another somewhere in the west of England. Deane's superiors were highly impressed; they clearly had found in Deane a man who knew his way around a conspiracy.

Feeble on Boon Island, powerless in St. Petersburg, John Deane now moved a nation. The British Ministry ordered the provisioning of ten thousand seamen for the following spring and kept thirty to forty ships of the lines at the ready to defend the Hanoverian Monarchy against the nefarious plot.

As it turned out, however, there was no invasion—Deane's great find was pure fantasy, the scheme was a product of the imagination, or possibly even a grand manipulation by Deane. There's no way of knowing. It was awfully convenient for Deane to have uncovered this alleged plot when he did—the captain's superiors were now thoroughly sold on him.

Deane was soon assigned to a British naval squadron as a sort of intelligence officer and spy master, dedicated to recruiting agents and gathering information regarding the movements and capabilities of the Russian Baltic fleet. He issued several reports on the strategic situation in the Baltic before returning to England by the fall of 1726.

Things were finally looking up for John Deane. He had powerful patrons, well pleased with his work, located at the highest reaches of the British government. Now it was just a question of time and positioning before the captain seized his next opportunity. First, though, it was time for a trip home to Wilford, to rest, renew relationships with family and old friends, and maybe gloat a little for all of his recent successes.

Local tradition has it that John and Jasper Deane had parted on bad terms when John Deane left for St. Petersburg in 1711. Now together again in the place of their boyhoods, the two brothers are said to have attempted reconciliation. A buoyant John Deane might have prattled on to his brother Jasper about his important friends, his adventures in Russia, his role in breaking a Jacobite spy ring and saving England, and his assignment providing intelligence on the movements of the Russian fleet. John Deane had become a person of note.

He must have expected at least a congratulations from Jasper, but his brother could take no pleasure in John's success. He was far past that. Jasper had sunk everything he could spare into the *Nottingham Galley* venture, and the terrible experience left him a broken man. He'd been forced to return to Wilford to farm, try and find peace, and rebuild his life on his family's ancestral lands, and, unlike his bachelor brother, he had a wife and children to care for. Jasper Deane seems to have lived simply, overseeing his flock of sheep.

But what could have been grated on him. He was the older brother, and for a time owned a promising little ship. He had laid the foundation of a rich merchant life, and he'd expected to play the major role in reestablishing the Deane family's social position. Jasper had agreed to let his younger brother captain his ship, only to see John ruin all of his dreams on the jagged rocks of New England. Not only was he unimpressed by John's successes, he was still bitter and resentful.

To John Deane, his brother's lack of appreciation was ungracious. Moreover it was outrageous and unforgivable that Jasper found fault with John and criticized him to his face and perhaps to others. John Deane understood that in life one necessarily made enemies, and he had them, in the Westminster halls of power, in Russia, and among the fast-disappearing sailors of the late *Nottingham Galley*.

But his own brother?

It was enough enemies for one man. On his visit home John and Jasper Deane got to arguing, things grew heated, and perhaps even physical. According to legend they were walking together after a party. No one knows if blows were struck, but they had a confrontation, and at some point Jasper burst a seam—the intense stress and emotional excitement of their disagreement caused a cerebral hemorrhage or heart attack.

And Jasper Deane dropped dead.

That's the folklore, and indeed Jasper Deane died in 1726, the year of his brother's return home, leaving an estate of £73, including twenty-two sheep, two pigs, one calf, and £35 in real estate. Over the course of his life he had just barely kept his head above water as his estate slowly sank. He left a widow, Elizabeth, and a daughter, Mary. If John Deane attended his brother's funeral, he shed no tears.

John Deane moved on and married a wealthy Warwickshire woman, Sarah, a moment that represented a major milestone for Deane in terms of both his personal and professional life. Little is known of his bride, except that she had money and is presumed to have been widowed, as she was only one year younger than Deane, who turned forty-six in 1726. Sarah was a catch for an aspiring gentleman like Deane, who was working hard at furthering his social position. But moreover, later events would suggest that Deane loved Sarah and that their marriage was a satisfying one.

For the first time in his life, John Deane had the emotional and financial support he craved, and he was able to use this foundation to plot and rebuild his career, which invariably involved self-promotion and a revival of his *Nottingham Galley Narrative*.

As always, John Deane sought to characterize the shipwreck story on his own terms. He rewrote, this time in the third person, what would become his final version. While adding a number of dramatic details, a few substantive additions stand out. Deane changed the ship's reported compass direction on the night of the wreck and made himself a more reluctant cannibal than in earlier versions. (Except that he includes an unusual anecdote—the gruesome story of how he tried to make a hand cream out of the fat of the dead carpenter.) He adds new stress to the barbarism of the common sailors, especially after the consumption of the Carpenter. And he furthers the image of himself as a tireless servant of the ship's company, always busy thatching the tent, looking for food, or personally changing the dressings on his sailors' wounds. In his final version, Captain Deane as nursemaid emerges as a major theme.

Lastly Deane addresses the issue of the dissension of Langman, Nicholas Mellen, and George White, although obliquely. He accuses his former crew of unspecified unchristian and immoral behavior while recovering in Portsmouth, and he also introduces the notion of some conflict on Boon Island, beginning on the third day of their marooning.

"As, after a shipwreck," declares Deane, "all Discipline and Command ceases, and all are reduc'd to a State of Equality; so that late Master [Deane himself] perceiving some refusing to give Assistance even when required in necessary Matters, he purposefully withdrew from the Society under the Pretense of collecting Materials for future Use, in order to give them a fair Opportunity of freely electing a Head, or Chief Commander."

Here, fifteen years after the fact, was the first time anyone ever mentioned an issue as significant to the shipwreck story as an election on Boon Island. Because it occurred on the third day, Deane separating himself from the crew is consistent with the social disintegration that usually occurs in the wake of a disaster. But there is something absurd about the idea of Deane isolating himself on such a small rock; he could only go so far. He said, "Returning one evening [as if he were by himself for several evenings?], he was inform'd by the People, that they had invested him with the same Powers, of issuing Orders, and Punishing any in Case of Disobedience, as before on board the Ship; and this they had enforced with stronger Sanction, in regard to some

Opposition made by the Mate and two others, against the Master's any longer enjoying Supreme Command."

It's Deane's one and only mention of dissension under his command. John Deane went on to work in the Foreign Office, again serving overseas, this time as His Majesty's Consul to the Ports of Flanders. And after ten years with the agency, and after a lifetime of careering, he finally retired. To celebrate, Deane once again published his shipwreck *Narrative,* a public testament to his superior character to accompany his superior wealth. By 1738 Deane had the means to retire with his wife Sarah in comfortable style. He built new adjacent houses in Wilford, and from there he managed his estate, which included lands and tenants.

Twenty-three years passed in relative peace, quiet, and maybe even happiness, but at last John Deane suffered a blow more devastating than the Boon Island winter or his public humiliation: Sarah passed away on August 17, 1761. Deane, while physiologically equipped to endure cold weather as a young man, was in his old age, powerless against a sudden emotional shock. He had built his world around her.

John Deane died the next day, on August 18, at the age of eighty-one.

Extraordinarily, even in death, John Deane found the means to carry on his lifelong battle against his enemies. In his will his wife Sarah would have received the support from the estate she brought into the marriage, and Deane's very elderly half sister was to get an annuity. And then John Deane's last will and testament turned at length to his niece, Mary Lorring, wife to an Edward Lorring, and daughter to his brother, Jasper Deane. John Deane left her the annual interest on £100, which was not an insignificant sum, but the language and terms were humiliating. Mary Lorring was to apply the money for "the use and maintenance of herself and her family and not embezel or waist it in fruitless and unnecessary expenses upon her own person." Furthermore, Mary Lorring and her family were not to give John Deane's wife or trustees "any Insult or trouble on their account and that the said Edward Lorring and said wife Mary or their children shall not reside or rome within forty miles of my said wife." If they did, then Sarah Deane and the other trustees had the right to cut off their inheritance.

John Deane found reasons to repeat again and again this sort of demeaning language throughout his lengthy ten-page will. Obviously Jasper Deane's daughter Mary shared her father's sense of grievance against her uncle and may have blamed him for her father's death. The Lorrings were likely harsh and unquiet critics of John Deane. Through his will John Deane sought to control their words and actions, and most of all, silence their criticisms.

Three hundred years later the captain's story continues to be heard. Captain Deane's *Narrative* has been published three times since his death, in 1917, 1968, and 1996. The story of the *Nottingham Galley* disaster appears in several shipwreck anthologies and is referenced in other tales of specific shipwrecks, particularly those involving cannibalism. In all of this literature the dissenting point of view of Langman, Mellen, and White is sometimes acknowledged but never thoroughly considered. (Though their entire *Account* was republished in the same volume as the latest version of Deane's story.)

History has been kind to Captain Deane, at least re-imaginings of it, as Deane has leapt off the *Nottingham Galley* and into the pages of fiction. In 1869 he was immortalized, certainly beyond his wildest imagination, as a swashbuckling hero in a novel penned by William Henry G. Kingston, entitled *John Deane of Nottingham*. Kingston's story features a young "Jack Deane," who, during the course of adventures from Sherwood Forest to the high seas, journeys from naive adolescence into manhood. The story references all the folklore associated with Deane, including his poaching, his running away to sea to serve and be promoted in the English Navy, his family's investment in the *Nottingham Galley,* his work as a spy in Russia, and the fight with and sudden death of his brother.

Kingston treats the Boon Island episode as an unrecognizable afterthought, in which the ship wrecks not in the winter off New England, but in a more benign season on an island somewhere in or around the New Jersey shore or Delaware Bay on its way to Pennsylvania. Kingston's book would appear to be of little value to anyone in search of the real John Deane, except for one striking theme, which in fact drives the entire story: In the first half of Kingston's fiction, John Deane becomes ensnared by Jacobites. He never really believes in their cause, but is lured into the Jacobite ring by a beautiful girl and cunning false friend. Guilty by association, Kingston's Jack Deane spends the rest of his life concealing his Jacobite history and redeeming himself in loyal service to his Protestant monarch, much like, as has been suggested here, the real John Deane seems to have actually done. Perhaps only one hundred years after John Deane's death, his reported suspicious activity off the coast of Ireland during the fatal voyage of the *Nottingham Galley*—and maybe also some dubious friendships or business relationships with known Jacobites—still lived in the collective memory of people residing in the vicinity of Nottingham and were accessible to Kingston when he wrote his novel.

A fictionalized John Deane appeared again in the twentieth century, when beloved American writer of historical novels Kenneth Roberts, author of such successful books as *Arundel, Rabble in Arms,* and *Northwest Passage,* wrote *Boon Island*, the final work of his prolific career. Published in 1955 to mixed reviews, Roberts's *Boon Island* charts a course very close to the story of the *Nottingham Galley*—as written by John Deane.

Like all of the larger-than-life heroes of Kenneth Roberts's work, the John Deane of *Boon Island* is a man of competence, common sense, and courage. Though not as widely read as his other books, the novel added the author's prestige (Roberts was featured on the cover of *Time* magazine in 1940) to Captain Deane's version of events.

Roberts felt no need to look seriously at the charges leveled by Deane's opponents. He was a master of detail throughout his career, including his early days as a journalist with the *Saturday Evening Post,* but he was less adept at approaching complex issues analytically or critically. His biographer, Jack Bales, noted, "While Roberts had the journalist's ability to research his articles, he seldom viewed any issue from more than one perspective, and rarely scrutinized the data to find the significance of the facts he had uncovered."

When interviewed about *Boon Island,* Roberts said of Langman that he "accused Deane of all sorts of impossible things." To Roberts, Langman was simply a "liar and a coward" who "hated Deane with an abysmal hatred," and that apparently was all the motivation Langman needed to concoct lies about Deane. And in the postscript of the novel, Roberts declares conclusively that "Captain John Deane so successfully defended himself against Langman's attacks that he was made His Majesty's Consul for the Ports of Flanders, residing at Ostend, and held his post for many years."

Kenneth Roberts was an even more aggressive advocate of John Deane than was John Deane himself, if one can imagine. Unlike either of the Deane brothers, he absolutely vilified Langman—every good story needs a villain. In his early days as a journalist, Roberts made a name for himself at the *Saturday Evening Post,* where he carried the banner of nativism—the author was rabidly anti-immigrant. Maybe it's not surprising, then, that Roberts's Langman was "a *swarthy* tall man with a dubious half-smile on one side of his mouth," part of his "snake-like" face.

Roberts's characterization of the *Nottingham Galley's* first mate is cartoonish, and Langman's malicious character is only tempered by his stupidity. He is "malice personified," a "whoreson, beetle-headed, flap-eared knave," guilty of "unreasoning hoggishness," and "always wrong," "with a "twisted mind" that "derided the truth, and defiled it." At one point in the novel, Miles Whitworth, a young gentleman and the voice of the story, laments, "There'll always be Langmans in this world, to set people and nations against each other—to condemn the good and extol the bad—to spread sly rumors and spit on the truth."

Roberts always drew his characters in bold black and white. An unapologetic elitist who had more sympathy for Benedict Arnold than for the ordinary citizen soldiers of the American Revolution, Roberts didn't need much convincing when it came to believing a sea captain and British diplomat over the pleadings of common sailors.

As for First Mate Christopher Langman, Boatswain Nicholas Mellen, and sailor George White, they made their stand against Captain Deane and his allies in London during the summer of 1711, and then all but disappeared into history. They left nothing behind except their printed words, testimonies of a horrible event, and charges against the man they held responsible.

Captain John Deane's long lifetime of writing and publishing allowed him to turn disaster, humiliation, and suspicion of treason into a calling card of courage, morality, and triumph. His many printed and written words survive along with the material remains from his life, including the two houses he built in his home village of Wilford, England, and his tomb at a nearby St. Wilfrid's churchyard. Of all the tombs in that churchyard, John Deane's stands out from the rest. It's the only one with an iron fence around it, as if to control the space around his final resting place, to keep enemies out, and secrets in.

Boon Island, unlike the other geography of the story—Portsmouth, New Hampshire; Boston; and London—is still recognizable as the place it was

three hundred years ago. The isle's position on the horizon as viewed from the mainland; its size, low-lying form, and out-lying ledges; and its soil-less and treeless nature are the same. The crags still make it difficult to walk on. The rainwater continues to turn brackish in its pools, and storms and tide, from time to time, wash over it. In winter the wind casts inevitable snow aloft off its sharp edges, blowing white powder against skies of bitter blue or somber gray. The waves pound relentlessly, but the rock is as unyielding as it was when fourteen hapless mariners were forced to lie on it.

The big change since the time of the *Nottingham Galley* wreck is the presence of a towering nineteenth-century granite lighthouse skewering the heart Boon Island. Erected to ward off ships from the island's treacherous ledges, it's the tallest lighthouse in New England. And a fitting memorial to the men who suffered so terribly on the cold rock there during the winter of 1710–1711.

Notes

PROLOGUE

"His Spirits still being in a Ferment . . ." Bales, Jack and Richard Warner, eds. *Boon Island: Including Contemporary Accounts of the Wreck of the* Nottingham Galley. Hanover, NH: University Press of New England. John Deane Account Revis'd, p. 80.

"with some difficulty got it out of the tent." Bales and Warner, p. 34.

"crept into the tent: again." Bales and Warner, p. 34.

"the Men began to request of [him] the dead Body to eat . . ." Bales and Warner, p. 34.

"so amazingly Shocking as this unexpected Proposal." Bales and Warner, p. 81.

"irresistible Vehemence." Bales and Warner, p. 81.

"with incessant Prayers and Tears," Bales and Warner, p. 81.

"the men called it 'beef.'" Bales and Warner, p. 82.

"this last Precaution was needless since they devoured it in a rapacious Manner . . ." Bales and Warner, p. 82.

CHAPTER 1

Population of York County, from *History of York County, Maine,* Clayton, W. Woodford. Philadelphia: Everts & Peck; 1880, p. 56.

Captain Lewis Bane's background: "The Genealogy and Family History of the State of Maine, Vol. I," Burrage, Henry Sweetser and Albert Roscoe Stubbs. New York: Lewis Historical Publishing Co.; 1909, p. 444, Capt. Lewis Bane was born on April 28, 1671 and died on June 25, 1721.

John Stover's history from Genealogy.com, Sylvester Stover family tree.

In Captain John Deane's *A Narrative of the Suffering, Preservation, and Deliverance of Capt. John Deane and Company; in the* Nottingham-Galley *of London, cast away on Boon Island, near New England, December 11, 1710,* Jasper Deane, ed. (London: R. Tooke, 1711), he places the corpse at a greater distance from the wreckage and mentions a paddle tied around the body's wrist. In *A True Account of the voyage of the* Nottingham-Galley *of London, John Deane Commander, from the River Thames to New England of First Mate Christopher Langman, Boatswain Nicholas Mellen, and sailor George White* (London: S. Popping, 1711), they refer to the second corpse up off the beach.

"Captain Deane was ready to be pulled through the waves by rope and buoy ..." The idea of using the rope and buoy to haul the captain through the water is only mentioned in Deane's first published *Narrative*, attached to a sermon published by Cotton Mather, "Compassions Called For: A Faithful Relation of some late but Strange Occurrences that call for an awful and useful Consideration. Especially the Surprising Distress and Deliverances of a Company lately shipwrecked on a Desolate Rock on the Coast of New England." Boston: Timothy Green, 1711.

"He was horrified by the captain's 'thin and meagre Aspect ...'" Bales and Warner, p. 84.

"He was perfectly affrighted at the Ghastly Figure . . ." Bales and Warner, p. 85.

"Still extremely weak, 'Deane had a very narrow escape from drowning,'" Bales and Warner, p. 37.

"The next morning early the Shallope by the Violence of the weather was drove on shore and cast away." From the appraisal of John Stover's shallop found among the Massachusetts Provincial Papers, House of Representatives, June 2, 1711. Also in *Documentary History of the State of Maine*, Vol. 9, Maine Historical Society, p. 299.

CHAPTER 2

"The sailor's appearance was 'to the terrible Affrightment of the Gentlewoman and her Children . . .' through 'restrained him from eating any more at that time.'" Bales and Warner, p. 87.

"but some 'strong Men, brought the rest, two or three at a time . . .'" Bales and Warner, p. 87.

"Though he was reduced to skin and bone, Deane considered himself as otherwise in 'perfect Health.'" Bales and Warner, p. 88.

"Mather made reference to men 'over-run with Ulcers,' 'starving to Death,' and 'Breaking on the Rock'" Mather, Cotton. "Compassions Called For: A Faithful Relation of some late but Strange Occurrences that call for an awful and useful Consideration. Especially the Surprising Distress and Deliverances of a Company lately shipwrecked on a Desolate Rock on the Coast of New England." Boston: Timothy Green, 1711.

"Which prompted the minster to write Penhallow for an account of 'the astonishing Example of outrageous wickedness among the strangers lately broke into your Neighborhood . . .'" And following quotes between Mather and Penhallow. Cotton Mather to Samuel Penhallow, January 1, 1710–1711. *Diary of Cotton Mather, Vol 2, 1709-24*. New York:

Frederick Ungar Publishing Co., pp 37-38. Mather must have written the wrong date on the letter. It clearly refers to the wreck of the *Nottingham Galley*, but news of the survivors did not reach the mainland until January 2.

"The Least material Mistake," he added, "may be a great Inconvenience . . . Write me then this week, a Letter that shall give me the Story with all the circumstances, which you think proper to have Exposed unto the World." Cotton Mather to Samuel Penhallow, 1 January 1710/11, in *Diary of Cotton Mather*, vol. 2, 1709–24 (New York: Frederick Ungar Publishing Co., 1957), pp. 37–38. Mather must have written the wrong date on the letter or held the letter for a few days and added more after dating it. It clearly refers to the wreck of the *Nottingham Galley*.

CHAPTER 3

"About Fifty feet in length and twelve foot abeam, give or take, with the wide-open decks and tall stern that characterized the galley . . ." A proportional measure of the *Nottingham Galley*'s dimensions can be estimated from the surviving plans of the larger 210 ton galley *Peregrine*, built at the English Deptford Dockyard in 1700.

"she had a shoal-form hull, flattened out at the bottom, which was useful in shallow waters, or when being rowed in dead-calm seas." Chapelle, Howard I. *The Search for Speed Under Sail*. London: Conway Maritime Press, 1968, pp. 33–38.

"When water froze, it could make the 'smallest rope in the ship as big as one's arm . . .'" Barlow, Edward. *Barlow's Journal: Of His Life at Sea in King's Ships; East and West Indiamen and Other Merchantmen from 1659–1703*. London: Hurst and Blackett, Ltd., p. 113.

"but, as Deane complained, 'contrary winds and bad weather' had slowed their progress." Bales and Warner, p. 24.

"(As Deane put it, he was 'slightly indisposed.')" Bales and Warner, p. 67.

"But to Deane's 'infinite sirprize . . .'" Bales and Warner, p. 67.

"The boat came to a sudden, crunching halt, hitting a ledge with 'great violence,'" Bales and Warner, p. 67.

"two vehement thumps upon the rock and a third . . ." Deane, Mather edition, 1710–1711.

"The Sea running so very high . . ." Deane, Mather edition, 1710–1711.

"The weather was so thick and Dark . . ." Bales and Warner, p. 24.

"Psychologists call this moment the 'period of impact.'" Leach, John. *Survival Psychology*. New York, New York: University Press, 1994, pp. 23–25.

". . . they prayed, 'earnestly supplicating Mercy.'" Bales and Warner, p. 67.

"Knowing Prayers without Endeavors are vain . . ." Bales and Warner, p. 25.

"Several su[n]ck so under racks of Conscience . . ." Bales and Warner, p. 25.

"cut by the board" Bales and Warner, p. 25.

"The mast 'Providently falling to the rock . . .'" Deane, Mather edition, 1710–1711.

"The fierceness of the wind . . ." Deane, Mather edition, 1710–1711.

"the Ship bulging, her decks opened . . ." Bales and Warner, p. 25.

"[I] hastened forward to prevent immediate perishing." Bales and Warner, p. 25.

CHAPTER 4

The earliest source of the Deane family history/folklore can be found in Mathew Henry Barker's *Walks around Nottingham by a Wanderer.* London: British Library, Historical Print Editions, 1835, pp. 49–51.

"At least one colony resorted to offering bounties . . ." *Newport History,* Volume 46 (4). Newport, RI: Newport Historical Society, 1973, pp. 81–85.

"Dairy products could easily take up the smaller spaces . . ." A sailor of the period, Edward Barlow, noted several times in his journal how much cheaper butter, cheese, and other provisions were in Ireland than they were in London. See Edward Barlow.

"The Navigation Acts in 1650 and 1651 . . ." MacDonald, William, Ed. *Select Charters and Other Documents Illustrative of American History, 1606–1775.* MacMillan Co., 1899, pp. 106–109.

CHAPTER 5

"Deane was 'heav'd with such Violence . . .'" Bales and Warner, p. 68.

"carried off again into the sea . . ." Bales and Warner, p. 68.

"preserving the use of his Reason," Bales and Warner, p. 68.

"he was able to drag himself 'into a place of Security before the next Revolution of the Sea.'" Bales and Warner, p. 68.

"There he collapsed, coughing, and vomiting seawater." Bales and Warner, p. 68.

"Deane knew this noting, 'with joyfull hearts we return'd humble thanks to Providence . . .'" Bales and Warner, p. 26.

"Maritime historian Peter Earle suggests that on any given voyage during this period, a merchant ship had a 3 to 5 percent chance of foundering." and subsequent Earle stats. Earle, Peter. *Sailors: English Merchant Seamen, 1650–1775.* London: Methuen Publishing, 1998, pp. 111–114.

"Another local shipwreck, this one a hundred years later on Isles of Shoals," "Wreck of the Seguntum." Town Records, Gossport, NH.

"At nearby Kittery, Maine, the average high temperatures for December and January are barely above freezing—34°F to 37°F (1°C to 3°C)—and the average low temperatures range from 14°F to 18°F (-8°C to -10°C)." Average temperatures compiled by the US Federal Research Division, Library of Congress.

"If exposure becomes serious enough, shivering will stop, indicating a serious case of hypothermia." Lloyd, Evan, M.D.. *Hypothermia and Cold Stress.* London: Croom Helm, 1986, p. 27.

"Normal body temperature averages 98.6°F (37°C) . . ." Wilkerson, James, Ed. "Human Body Temperature and its Control," *Hypothermia, Frostbite and Other Cold Injuries.* Seattle: Mountaineers, 1986.

"Core temperatures below this point are fatal if allowed to continue untreated." Lloyd, p. 25.

"As Deane explained it, the weather still continuing extream cold, with Snow and Rain." Bales and Warner, p. 26.

In the case of another ship, the *Invercauld,* which wrecked on the sub-Antarctic island of Auckland in 1864, the captain and mate found that the density and awkward bulk of their heavy coats endangered them in the water, but on land these coats probably saved their lives. Of the nineteen men who escaped the *Invercauld* to make it to shore, only three survived their cold confinement on Auckland Island, and two of these were the captain and the mate with their coats. See Druett, Joan. *Island of the Lost.* Chapel Hill. Algonquin Books, 2007. The *Invercauld* survivors also had access to fire, a big advantage over the *Nottingham Galley* castaways.

"without a Shovel full of Earth and destitute of the Growth of a single Shrub." Bales and Warner, p. 68.

"so very craggy that we coul'd not walk to keep our selves warm, as the captain recalled." Bales and Warner, p. 26.

"Layers of softer and harder rock, some more resistant to erosion than others . . ." Correspondence with Robert Marvinney, Director of the Maine Geological Survey and State Geologist.

"In this 'disconsolate Condition they spent the first miserable Night.'" Bales and Warner, p. 69.

CHAPTER 6
"When the Day appeared, it presented us with a dismal Spectacle, a doleful little Spot in the Sea . . ." Deane, Mather edition, 1710–1711.

"Drill of very swift Motion." Bales and Warner, p. 69.

"The men 'stow'd one upon another, under the Canvas, . . .'" Bales and Warner, p. 69.

"'with the Hopes of being discover'd by Fishing Shallops, . . .'" Bales and Warner, p. 69.

"The task was apparently too much for at least four members of the crew who were unresponsive and lethargic . . ." Bales and Warner, p. 70.

"The time immediately following an extremely stressful event is often characterized by 'confusion' and 'social fragmentation.' During the

first couple of days after a disaster, survivors often experience 'denial and apathy.'" Leach, pp. 126–134.

"Among those not working was Downs, the cook, who had finally put down the flint and steel and now complained 'he was almost starved.'" Bales and Warner, p. 27.

"If the cheese was at this time floating in the surf, the survivors were not yet desperate enough to eat it, for it had been 'beaten into uncouth Forms by the violent Dashing of the Sea against the Rock.'" Bales and Warner, p. 69.

"'Our Cook, unused to the Hardships of a sea-faring Life,' recalled the captain ..." Bales and Warner, p. 69.

"As the body makes these adjustments during the first three days of cold exposure, 'there is a temporary continuous increase in venous pressure and this sudden surge of blood may cause overloading and failure of a vulnerable heart.'" Lloyd, Evan, M.D., p. 103. Bangs, Cameron C. "Response to Cooling." *Hypothermia, Frostbite, and Other Cold Injuries.* Seattle: Mountaineers Books, pp. 41–42.

Nearly anyone could get hired on as a ship's cook, especially in wartime when there were shortages of sailors. Redicker, Marcus. *Between the Devil and the Deep Blue Sea: Merchant Seamen, Pirates and the Anglo-American Maritime World, 1700–1750.* Cambridge, UK: Cambridge University Press. 1987, pp. 85, 123.

"'Several with my self afterwards aknowledged, had thot's of it,' explained Deane." Bales and Warner, p. 27.

"According to Captain Deane, 'The rest of our Men were generally so ill and bruised,' two days after the wreck, "that but 4 or 5 of us were able to attempt anything for our safety." Deane, Mather edition, 1710–1711.

"They began to methodically scavenge the Boon Island coastline, finding 'more Planks and Canvass sent us a shoar,' and these they used to build a tent, 'in a Triangular form.'" Deane, Mather edition, 1710–1711.

"where we housed ourselves from Wind and Weather." Deane, Mather edition, 1710–1711.

Similar structures used in mountain rescue situations have the same effect. Evan Lloyd, M.D., a specialist in cold weather medicine, believes the tent was the key to survival on Boon Island. Correspondence with Evan Lloyd, M.D., September 2008.

"'The sea Flowing high, came into our Tent, and carry'd away part of it,' recalled Deane . . ." Deane, Mather edition, 1710–1711.

"The captain explained that he drew yarn from rope and with it 'thatched the tent,' which could 'turn off 2 or 3 Hours of Rain . . .'" Bales and Warner, p. 79.

"Deane noted that it was 'extream cold' on the third day, . . ." Bales and Warner, p. 27.

"Deane and his men were keenly aware of—and very frightened by—this 'mortification' of flesh. Bales and Warner, p. 71.

CHAPTER 7

"They piled up assorted timbers and planking, pulled nails out of old sheeting, and collected oakum, sheet lead, long pieces of canvas, pump leather, and some new 'Holland Duck,' a high-quality sailcloth." Bales and Warner, p. 28.

"As Captain John Deane explained, spying the ships 'rejoyced us not a little.'" Bales and Warner, p. 28.

"'We receiv'd no small encouragement from the sight of 'em,' Deane recalled. '[It] gave us reason to conclude our distress might be known...'" Bales and Warner, p. 28.

"It grew 'so extream cold that we could seldom stay out of the Tent above four hours in the day,' he [Deane] explained, 'and some days do nothing at all.'" Bales and Warner, p. 28.

"thro' a violent Indisposition, [he] was utterly incapacitated from giving his necessary Assistance (and) almost his advice." Bales and Warner, p. 72.

"Every evening in the noxious confines of their shelter, Captain Deane would move among his men in the cramped quarters of the tent, and 'daily dress'd their Ulcers,'..." Bales and Warner, p. 71.

"Unbeknownst to the crew, however, they were shedding not only excess fluids when they relieved themselves, but they were also losing some of their precious core heat, as urination is yet another means of heat loss." Lloyd, p. 20.

"After dousing themselves, they bound up their wounds again 'in Clean Rags, supplied from two Pieces of Linnen, amongst other Things, driven on Shore.' And they, 'wrapp'd up their Legs in large swathing Bands of Oakum, pick'd and dried for that Purpose.'" Bales and Warner, p. 71.

"'In regard to fresh water,' noted Deane, they were 'indifferently well supplied all of the Time by Rain, and melted Snow lodging in the concavities of the highest Part of the Rock,'..." Bales and Warner. pp. 78–79.

"Occasionally drinking slightly salinated water, or even straight sea-water, would have no serious medical effects." Bombard, Alain, *The Bombard Story*. London: Grafton: 1986. To test his many survival theories Bombard placed himself on a raft of his own design and drifted across the Atlantic. Among his discoveries was that humans could drink a quart of seawater per day for a period of time without harm, so long as the consumption of seawater did not begin after a prolonged period of dehydration.

"Dehydration compounds the threat from frostbite . . ." Lloyd, p. 85.

"According to Deane this jostling was responsible for 'occasioning some disputes.'" Bales and Warner. p. 71.

"In the first stage of a pressure sore, the skin simply appears bruised." and following. *Journal of the American Medical Association.* August 23–30, 2006.

"With their painful sores, tight quarters, lack of privacy, hard rock, and the cold, sleep deprivation became an issue." Lloyd, pp. 31–34.

"The captain described most of the ships' company as 'so benumb'd and feeble as not able to stir.'" Bales and Warner, p. 28.

"What's more, extra body fat usually means a person is less fit, and the unfit are usually the first to perish, which was likely the case with Martin Downs, the ship's cook." Wilkerson, James, Ed. "Avoiding Hypothermia," *Hypothermia, Frostbite and Other Cold Injuries.* Seattle: Mountaineers, 1986.

"Deane stated that the ax was a present that 'Providence so ordered.'" Bales and Warner, p. 29.

"'I offering my self as one to adventure, which they agreed to, because I was the strongest, and therefore fittest to undergo the extremities we might be reduc'd to,' Deane explained . . ." Bales and Warner, p. 29.

"As Deane recalled: 'The swell of the Sea heav'd her along shore, and overset her upon us. . .'" Bales and Warner, p. 29.

"Deane, in hindsight, was able to find some consolation, pointing out that 'had we been at Sea in that imitation of a boat, . . .'" Bales and Warner, p. 29.

"We were now reduc'd to the most deplorable and mallancholy Circumstances imaginable, almost every Man but myself, weak to an extremity, and near starved with Hunger and Cold . . ." Bales and Warner, pp. 29–30.

CHAPTER 8

"Captain John Deane and his men were right to worry that the ocean would rise to cover the island—waves have washed over Boon before . . ." Molloy Porter, Jane. *Friendly Edifices: Piscataqua Lighthouses and Other Aids to Navigation, 1771–1939.* Portsmouth Marine Society, p. 348.

"'I have gone myself (no other Person being able) several days at low water,' he recalled, 'and could get no more than two or three at Piece, . . .'" Bales and Warner, p. 32.

"It got so bad with the rising waters that, finding little rockweed, Deane brought a piece of 'green hide being thrown up by the sea (fasten'd to a piece of the Main-Yard)' . . ." Bales and Warner, p. 32.

"They had to eat the bird raw, and it was on the small side, 'scarce every one a mouthful,' Captain Deane noted, . . ." Bales and Warner, p. 32.

"For his extra work Deane 'reap'd one Benefit, for maintaining of Warmth by Action, preserv'd a due Circulation of Blood, imparting a benign Influence to the whole System.'" Bales and Warner, p. 71.

"The rate of survival in cold weather situations can be directly related to body mass." and following. Wilkerson, pp. 6–7.

"No matter where it resides, the human body has evolved to defend itself from the cold." and following. Wilkerson, pp. 8–9, 85–86.

"Various other chemical and physiological differences can enhance functioning and survival in cold weather, too." and following. Wilkerson, p. 86.

"As the weeks passed, Captain Deane watched the bodies of his men break down." and following. Russell, Sharman Apt. *Hunger: An Unnatural History.* New York, New York: University Press, 1994, pp. 37–39.

"Most people can live for about sixty days without food." and following. Russell, page 107. Leach, p. 92.

"Similarly, other research has shown a calorie-deprived man wearing two suits and two topcoats in the middle of summer and still unable to keep warm." Roland, Charles G. *Courage Under Siege.* New York: Oxford Press, 1992, p. 116.

"From the beginning, the sailor the captain called 'a stout, brave Fellow' . . ." Bales and Warner, p. 31.

"The construction of the raft, as the captain described it, would have to be accomplished 'without Tools, and, almost without Hands.'" Bales and Warner, p. 75.

"Studies have shown that when hand surface temperature reaches 55°F (12.8°C), manual performance begins to become impaired." Lockhart, John M. "Effects of Body and Hand Cooling on Complex Manual Performance," *Journal of Applied Psychology.* Vol. 50 (1066), pp. 57–59.

"After that he managed to split the twelve-foot foreyard down the middle and joined the two pieces together by thin, four-foot-long planks, 'first Spiking, then seizing them firm.'" Bales and Warner, p. 75.

"The captain, 'deliberately weighing the Difficulties of the Adventure, judg'd them, rationally speaking, unsurmountable, ...'" Bales and Warner, p. 76.

"According to Deane, the first mate was vehement and unequivocal—he 'strenuously oppos'd it, on account 'twas so late (being 2 in the afternoon).'" Bales and Warner, p. 31.

"'Committing the enterprise to God's Blessing,' the Swede was placed on the raft, since he couldn't wade into the water on his incapacitated legs." Bales and Warner, p. 31.

"'The Swell, rowling very high, soon overset them as it did our boat,' the captain recalled." Bales and Warner, p. 31.

"But, Deane explained, the other man struggled, 'being no swimmer,' so the captain dove in and dragged the drowning sailor back to the rock." Bales and Warner, pp. 31–32.

"As Captain Deane put it, the sign of smoke was 'interpreted by them as a Token of speedy Deliverance. This Flush of Hope, Under God, subserv'd for a Time to support them.'" Bales and Warner, p. 78.

CHAPTER 9
"Forty-seven years old, 'a fat Man, and naturally of a dull, heavy, Phlegmatick Constitution and Disposition,' according to Captain John Deane ..." Bales and Warner, p. 79.

"He was in even worse shape than he knew." and following. Correspondence with Evan Lloyd, M.D., October 2008.

"The Captain said that they prayed over the Carpenter and did what they could to help him, but he became incommunicable, 'sensible tho' speechless.'" Bales and Warner, p. 33.

"enquired of them that lay next to him, who told me, he was dead." Deane, Mather edition, 1710–1711.

"As Deane put it, they 'suffered the Body to remain with us 'till morning.'" Bales and Warner, p. 33.

"Lack of food causes 'apathy, depression, emotional instability, and impairment of concentration and memory.'" Leach, p. 90.

"Victims of starvation can begin to lose their humanity and behave as 'wild beasts.'" Leach, pp. 88–89.

"On his way out he made it known that he 'desir'd them who were best able to remove it [the body].'" Bales and Warner, p. 34.

"Someone must have offered to help him, because he explained that 'with some difficulty we got it out of the tent.'" Bales and Warner, p. 34.

"During the Crusades, word arrived back in Europe that starving Crusaders had been forced to consume Saracens." Price, Merrall Llewelyn. *Consuming Passions: The Uses of Cannibalism in Late Medieval and Early Modern Europe.* New York: Routledge Press, 2003, pp. 5–18.

"Furthermore, if someone had to die and be eaten so that others might live, killing became legal as long as it was done by drawing lots, a tradition that goes back to the Hebrew Testament story of Jonah." Jonah 1:7.

"But from a cultural and visceral point of view, the notion that man eating is an unnatural and repulsive act under any circumstance persisted in Western society." Avramescu, Catalin. *An Intellectual History of Cannibalism.* Princeton, NJ: Princeton University Press, 2009, pp. 5–40.

"The idea of eating the Carpenter was, as Captain Deane claimed, 'most grievous and shocking,' and it prompted a lengthy debate about 'lawfullness and sinfulness on the one Hand; and absolute Necessity on the other.'" Bales and Warner, p. 34.

"Several men . . . wanted no part of it, calling '(eating the Carpenter) a heinous Sin.'" Bales and Warner, p. 80.

"Two men had by this time died on the island, at least in part from starvation, and two others were lost on the raft, and the rest, it was argued, were at their 'last Exreamity.'" Bales and Warner, p. 34.

"Judgment, Conscience, &c. were oblig'd to submit to the more prevailing arguments of our craving appetites." Bales and Warner, p. 34.

"After 'maturely weighing all Circumstances, pronounc'd in Favor of the Majority, arguing the improbability of it being a Sin to eat Humane Flesh in case of such necessity, provided they were no ways accessary to the taking away of Life.'" Bales and Warner, p. 81.

"'I then cut part of the flesh in thin Slices, and washing it in the saltwater, brought it to the Tent, and oblig'd the men to eat Rockweed along with it, to serve instead of bread.' That night most of them ate the gruesome meal but those who had stood their ground and refused. By morning, however, these dissenters had changed their minds, and, as Deane noted, 'earnestly desir'd to partake with the rest.'" Bales and Warner, pp. 34–35.

"I found (in a few days) their very natural dispositions chang'd, and that affectionate, peaceable temper they had all along hitherto discover'd totally lost; . . ." Bales and Warner, p. 35.

"The captain did his best to guard and ration the meat, but he worried what would happen once it was gone. Immediate rescue was necessary, lest 'we be forc'd to feed upon the living: which we must certainly have done, had we staid a few days longer.'" Bales and Warner, p. 35.

"Studies have shown that barbarism seems to naturally follow cannibalism . . ." and following. Leach, pp. 88–92.

"He said it had 'an ill Effect about their Ulcers and Sores, endangering a Mortification more than ever.'" Bales and Warner, p. 82.

"From the tent everyone, no matter how weak and infirm, 'instantly thrust out his Head to see so desirable Sight and to express the Raptures diffus'd throughout the whole Company, upon the Prospect of so sudden and unexpected a Deliverance. . .'twas Life from the Dead.'" Bales and Warner, p. 82.

"Expectations of Deliverance, and fears of miscarriage, hurry'd our weak and disorder'd spirits strangely." Bales and Warner, p. 36.

Though they were all starving—with only the remainders of the human carcass left to eat—the captain apparently wished to manage the situation in such a way that deprioritized food. Bales and Warner, p. 36.

"Our flesh so wasted, and our looks so ghastly and frightful, that it was really a very dismal prospect." Bales and Warner, p. 36.

"'Twas a very uncomfortable sight,' Deane remembered, 'to see our worthy friends in the Shallop stand away from shore without us. ... had we been with them, we must have perish'd, not having sufficient strength to help ourselves." Bales and Warner, p. 37.

"The next day our Men urging me vehemently for more flesh, I gave them a little more than usual, but not to their satisfaction, for they wou'd certainly have eat up the whole at once." Bales and Warner, p. 37.

CHAPTER 10
As Langman recalled: "several of us had our Legs so frozen, and were so weak that we could not walk." Bales and Warner, p. 56.

"These gentlemen took great care of us, and would not suffer us to eat or drink but a little at time, lest it should do us hurt." Bales and Warner, pp. 56–57.

"'Night we arrived at Piscataqua in New England,'" Langman remembered, "'where we were all provided for.'" Bales and Warner, p. 57.

"'[had] a Doctor appointed to look after us,' Langman noted gratefully." Bales and Warner, p. 57.

"He easily acquired the first, stopping by Langman's side and imploring the mate—who was still 'very ill of a Flux and Fever . . .'" Bales and Warner, p. 57.

"Then something curious happened. George White, who had never before been referred to as boatswain, and who was also very unwell, signed as the boatswain." Bales and Warner, p. 57.

"White explained later that he signed the protest 'for fear of being put of out his Lodgings by the Captain, while he was both sick and lame.'" Bales and Warner, p. 57.

"He terrified the Furber family on that night, and according to Langman, he scared the Furber children further during his stay, telling them 'he would have made a Frigasy out of them, if he had had 'em in Boon Island.' With tales like this, the first mate said, Captain Deane 'frighten'd the People that heard him; and made them esteem him as a Brute, as he was.'" Bales and Warner, p. 58.

"'Instead of being thankful to God for his own and our Deliverance, he returned with the Dog to his Vomit, and behav'd himself so brutishly, that his Friend Captain Furber was obliged to turn him out of his House,' remembered Langman, Mellen, and White." Bales and Warner, p. 58.

"The Captain, they said, 'compell'd us to sign what our Illness made us uncapable to understand.'" Bales and Warner, p. 43.

"Two of them had signed the captain's protest but now wished to disavow their endorsement of Deane's version of the events, calling the document 'false, and Hardly a word of Truth in it.'" Bales and Warner, p. 60.

"But he had developed a reputation as being fair and just, 'charitable to the poor and hospitable to strangers.'" The judge was considered "prompt and firm" and "literally a terror to evil-doers," Giddings, Edward Jonathan. *American Christian Rulers.* New York: Broadfield and Co., 1889, p. 365.

"Christopher Langman, Nicholas Mellin [*sic*], and George White, personally appeared before me the Subscriber . . ." Bales and Warner, p. 61.

"As Langman put it: 'He likewise wrong'd us of what the Good People gave us towards our relief, and applied it to his own and his Brother's Use." Bales and Warner, p. 58.

"When Captain John Wentworth gave several of our Men good Cloaths, Captain Deane came and order'd them the worst that could be had." Bales and Warner, p. 58.

"Deane's behavior, said Langman, was 'so barbarous as to get us turn'd out of our lodgings, before we were able to shift for our selves.'" Bales and Warner, p. 58.

"'The Captain had reason indeed to commend the Charity of the Gentlemen of New England,' say Langman, Mellen and White . . ." Bales and Warner, p. 44.

According to Langman, Mellen, and White, the men were kicked out of the tavern before they were able to fend for themselves. They are not specific in the timing of what came first—their eviction or their meeting with Penhallow. In other words, did the captain get them evicted because they were not cooperating? Did they go to the judge because they were angry about being turned out of their lodging? It's unknown which came first.

CHAPTER 11

"First was the ship's company itself—the vessel had a crew of fourteen, just as Captain John Deane had said, but able seamen they all were not. According to the trio, 'not above 6 of the men were capable to Serve in the Ship, in case of bad Weather.'" Bales and Warner, p. 45.

"The grievance of having too few hands aboard was a frequent complaint and sometimes one of the reasons given for mutiny." Rediker, p. 228.

"Not only did impressment drive up the demand for sailors, but it also sent sailors fleeing inland to avoid the gangs, further aggravating the shortage of crewmen." Earle, pp. 199–201.

"Seaman often signed onto merchant vessels for the sole purpose of escaping the gangs, preferring the money they could make in the private sector over life as a navy man." and following. Rediker, p. 122.

"The ship may have had ten guns aboard, and one man designated as a gunner, but, as Langman and his two allies pointed out, four of these cannon were 'useless,' . . ." Bales and Warner, p. 45.

"The ship met the parade at an area near the sandbank at the mouth of the Thames called 'the Nore,' and they took a position 'off of Whitby' and 'brought to' when a storm blew in." Bales and Warner, p. 45.

"Then, according to Mellen, White, and Langman, Captain Deane took what appeared to be a calculated risk by breaking from the Navy's protection and making a run up over Scotland past the Shetland Islands to Northern Ireland in what was described as a 'fine gale.'" Bales and Warner, p. 45. This route is only slightly longer than sailing from London to Cornwall, then turning north past the Isle of Man.

"During the wars that raged between England and France from 1695 and to 1713, French corsairs took ten thousand ships, half to three quarters of which were English." Earle, p. 120.

By leaving the protection of the convoy, Captain Deane took a calculated risk. Barlow records East India merchant ships forced to run aground in Ireland and three more captured by French privateers in 1695.

"Captain Deane was evidently unconcerned about the two ships that lay in the path of the *Nottingham Galley* and 'would have bore down (on them) . . .' claimed Langman, Mellen, and White." Bales and Warner, p. 45.

"They continued, '. . . but the Men would not consent to it, because they perceiv'd them [the two vessels lying ahead] to be French men-of-war.'" Bales and Warner, p. 45.

"It was not uncommon for a merchant captain to consult with his men when faced with the choice of standing and fighting, running, or surrendering." Earle, in *Sailors: English Merchant Seamen, 1650–1775*, writes: "Usually the men in a threatened ship would realize their situation sooner or later and then the Captain had to decide, often in consultation with his crew, whether to run, stand and fight, or most common, stand and surrender at once since the odds were usually hopelessly against the merchant ship." Also, see the advantages of privateers, pp. 120–121.

"In the parlance of the time, anything from a minor questioning of authority to open revolt might be considered 'mutiny.'" Earle on definitions of *mutiny*, p. 175.

"And perhaps that's all it was, since the disagreement went on as the alien vessels chased the *Nottingham Galley* 'for about the Space of three Leagues' during which time Deane 'often would have bore down upon them' if it were not for the objections, or resistance, of 'the men.'" Bales and Warner, p. 61.

"Upon this we stood off to Sea until 12 at Night, when the Captain, coming upon Deck, we Sail'd easily in toward the shore, by the Mate's

Advice, 'till Daylight, and came so near land that we were forced to stand off." Bales and Warner, p. 45.

"Langman, Mellen, and White reported that the 'next Day we saw the two Privateers again, and the Captain propos'd to stand down toward them, or to come to.'" Bales and Warner, p. 45.

"The merchant told the Captain 'that he would rather the said Ship would be lost than obtain her design'd Port in Safety, having made £200 Insurance.'" Bales and Warner, p. 45.

"Captain Deane responded that 'his brother Jasper Deane had made £300 insurance and immediately after said, if he thought he could secure the Insurance he would run the Ship on Shore,' a common practice against privateers in an otherwise hopeless situation." Bales and Warner, p. 62. On purposefully running ashore, see Earle, p. 121.

"Seaman White heard the same thing. He noted that he was within earshot on the previous day, when Whitworth had said 'that he had rather be taken than not'..." Bales and Warner, pp. 59, 62.

"A historian of Lloyd's Coffee House points that one could obtain insurance for just about anything including truthfulness, marriage, chastity, the long life of horses, or even protection from 'death by drinking in Geneva.'" Straus, Ralph. *Lloyd's: The Gentlemen of the Coffee-House.* New York: Carrick and Evans, 1938, p. 27.

"In one noteworthy example before the war with France, a master tried to bribe the pilot with drink as they entered a French port so that he would look the other way when the ship was run aground." and following. Straus, p. 50.

"These were put into a chest, and he 'commanded the men to carry them into the Boat, which they did.'" Bales and Warner, p. 46.

"As one seaman of the period pointed out, men in just this type of situation could lose 'more in a moment than they can get again, maybe in all their life time.'" Barlow, p. 226.

"A typical sailor would carry aboard multiple changes of clothing including shirts, a jacket, breeches, stockings, shoes, woolen gloves, a 'whapping large watch-coat, cloak or military campaign coat,' and a flat, round hat called a 'Monmouth cap,' or 'mountaineers' or 'hunters' cap with ear flaps." and following. Barlow, p. 226.

"All of this added up." and the following paragraph. Earle on the outfitting of sailor, pp. 34–35. Rediker, p. 123.

"As was the tradition in trans-Atlantic voyages, the crew had presumably already received a month's pay at Gravesend. (Crews were paid this portion of their wages after the ship was loaded and underway to keep them from jumping ship while still in port.)" The two principle authorities on English merchant seamen do not seem agree on whether or not ship insurance covered sailors' wages. Marcus Rediker, in his book, *Between the Devil and the Deep Blue Sea*, states that knowledge that the ship was insured constituted a "situation that guaranteed their wages," p. 120. But Peter Earle, in *Sailors: English Merchant Seamen, 1650–1775*, contends more logically that insurance did not cover sailor's wages out of concern that they might not sufficiently defend their ship if they could as easily get paid by surrendering as not. See Earle, pp. 32, 111, 121.

"On the other hand, if they rebelled against the captain, they risked both punishment and loss of wages." According to Rediker, "If a sailor be mutinous, disobedient, or dessert the ship, he makes total forfeiture of all of his wages," p. 120.

"John Deane was a man who valued and demanded personal loyalty, and in exchange he 'promis'd that we should want for nothing,' according to Langman, Mellen, and White." Bales and Warner, p. 46.

"As the boatswain and the other men followed the captain's instructions, they all 'plainly saw that he resolv'd to lose the Ship.'" Bales and Warner, p. 46.

"As the men described it: 'He [Captain Deane] was opposed by Mate Christopher Langman, who wrought the Vessel through between the Main and an Island, and she arrived safely at Killybags in Ireland that same Night." Bales and Warner, p. 46.

"The Master the next Day would have gone ashore and left the Ship, and put a Chest and several other things in the Boat." and following. Bales and Warner, p. 59.

"Recorded mutinies were relatively rare—and always dangerous propositions." and following. Earle, pp. 175–182. Only nine mutinies were reported during the war years of 1702–1713, 1727, and 1740–1748. During wartime, wages were higher and sailors were subject to the stricter discipline of the Royal Navy. Not only was a rebellion against a captain seen as mutiny, but it also was akin to treason when the nation was in peril, making the crime even less acceptable.

"Take the case of the *Haswell*, which was on its way to Virginia in 1735 when the boatswain led the crew in an uprising and 'murdered the master and his mates in a most barbarous manner.'" Earle, p. 180.

The best-known mutinies were bloody, but removing the captain from control of a ship could also be nonviolent, as illustrated by cases more analogous to the circumstances claimed by Langman, Mellen, and White." and following. Earle, p. 178.

"Mutiny usually formed around a nucleus of rebels, and they could succeed with as few as 20 percent of the ship's company participating, so long as the remaining 80 percent of the crew were neutral." Rediker, pp. 228–229.

Chapter 12

Traditions—and even law—held that once at sea a ship's captain was all powerful. and following. Rediker, pp. 159–160.

"Captain Deane, 'by his barbarous Treatment of our Men,' they claimed, 'had disabled several of 'em.'" and **"Two of our best Sailors were so unmercifully beat by him, because they oppos'd his Design above mentioned, that they were not able to work in a Month."** Bales and Warner, p. 46.

"The nature of a captain's authority aboard ship was a personal matter." and following. Earle, p. 178.

"He pulled the man from his hammock 'by the hair of his head & told him he would be his Doctor and with great violence gave him upwards of sixty blows over his head, eyes, face, mouth and breast & knocked and beat his head against the cable.'" The story is quoted in Rediker, p. 225. See also Earle on using incapacity as evidence of excessive discipline, p 153.

"'Besides,' they claimed, 'he put us to short Allowance, so that we had but one Quart of Water per Head in twenty four Hours, and had nothing to eat but salt Beef, which made us so dry that we were forc'd to drink the Rain water that run off the Deck.'" Bales and Warner, p. 46.

"Upon finding the hold open, he went below for 'a Gallon of water to Quench our Thirst.' Captain Deane discovered the attempt and 'knocked down' the man, leaving him 'for dead.'" Bales and Warner, p. 46.

"And when the master of the ship was part owner, complaints about the low quality and quantity of food were more common, since the more money saved in provisioning the ship, the more money went into the owner's pocket." Rediker, p. 222.

On larger vessels, Edward Barlow reported, "poor seaman [are] many times abused by pursers and stewards" who skim money off the top while sailors half starve with unsavory victuals. As an illustration, Barlow urged his readers to "take a peck of malt and heave it over London Bridge and let it wash or swim down the Thames to Gravesend and then take it up! It would be much better beer than we drunk. Barlow, pp. 127–128.

The dissenters said that while the captain 'pretended to us that he confin'd himself also to short Allowences yet we knew the contrary' and that he 'wanted nothing himself.'" Bales and Warner, p. 46.

"Captain Deane attributed the ship's slow voyage to 'contrary winds,' but Langman, Mellen, and White blamed it on the debilitation of a crew who was riddled with landsmen, weakened by being kept on short allowances, and crippled by the hand of their own captain." Bales and Warner, p. 24.

"No sooner had they entered Canadian waters than a ship was sighted in the distance, making for the *Nottingham Galley* 'with all the Sail she could.'" Bales and Warner, p. 46.

Such was the case of the *Illustrious*, a galley with about the same armament as the *Nottingham Galley*, but with a crew of 120 men packed aboard." and following. *Boston News Letter,* September 10–17, 1711.

("One notable sea captain of the period said, 'Good Liquor to sailors is preferable to clothing.'") Woodes Rogers, quoted in Rediker, p. 191.

"The ship they encountered was the 'Pompey Galley of London, Captain Den Commander, at which we rejoic'd, tho our Captain was melancholy,' . . ." Bales and Warner, p. 47.

"Continuing on toward New England, the crew finally sighted land at Cape Sables, the southern tip of Acadia, the future Nova Scotia, which had just been taken from the French by the English." See

Francis Parkman, *Montcalm and Wolfe*. Boston: Little, Brown and Co., 1901, pp. 522–524.

"By the following spring, however, the *Boston News Letter* would report an English sloop taken by 'a large privateer Sloop of 40 men,' . . ." *Boston News Letter*, April 1711.

"As the storm grew worse on the evening of December 10, they were forced to 'hand all our Sails and, and lie under our Mizzen-Ballast till Daylight.'" Bales and Warner, p. 47.

"According to Langman and Mellen, the captain baldly stated that this was the first land they had yet seen, 'wherein he was justly contradicted by the Mate, which caus'd some Words between 'em: For in Truth we had made Cape Sables a week before.'" Bales and Warner, p. 47.

"The fate of the *Nottingham Galley* seems to have hinged upon that delay. Had they stayed on their original course, 'According to the Opinion of the Mate and the Ship's Company, we had, in all probability, arriv'd safe the next Day at Boston.'" Bales and Warner, p. 47.

CHAPTER 13

"'(N)ot one Man was hurt in getting ashore,' said Christopher Langman, Nicholas Mellen, and George White. Neither did the captain almost drown in his epic escape during the storm-tossed night. The seas washing over the ledge were shallow: 'no deeper,' according to the three deponents, 'than our Middle.'" Bales and Warner, p. 50.

"When they were launching the craft, the three sailors said, 'some Controversie happ'd who the six [on board] should be,' and the decision seems to have been based on who could best lay claim to the boat. The Carpenter 'pleaded his Right' because he built it." Bales and Warner, p. 52.

"The pair 'held the Boat almost an Hour with a rope in Hopes to save her till the Weather grew more calm.'" Bales and Warner, p. 52.

"When the 'Swede' was ready to launch *his* raft, the trio contend that he never asked the captain to accompany him, and the captain made no offer to, saying instead, 'Let who will go t'was all one to him.'" Bales and Warner, p. 54.

"'Tis likewise false, that the Captain went several times out to look for Provisions, for George White was always with him . . ." Bales and Warner, pp. 54–55.

"Langman, Mellen, and White reported that they, 'could see Houses on the main Land, and several Boats rowing to and fro', which rejoic'd us very much.'" Bales and Warner, p. 52.

"Captain Deane's relative health kept him from sharing in these delusions." Lloyd, p. 141.

"It was Captain Deane, they said, who first proposed cannibalizing the Carpenter, arguing 'It was no Sin, since God was pleas'd to take him out of the World, and that we had not laid violent Hands upon him . . .'" Bales and Warner, p. 54.

"[T]he Captain's Pretensions of being moved with Horror at the Thoughts of it, are false, for there was no Man that eat more of the Corps than himself." Bales and Warner, p. 55.

"I found they all eat abundance and with the utmost greediness, so that I was constrain'd to carry the quarters farther from the Tent, (quite out of their Reach) least they shou'd prejudice themselves by overmuch eating, as also expend our small stock too soon." Bales and Warner, p. 35.

"'It was likewise false,' they said, 'that any of the men removed the Dead body from the Place where they laid it at first.'" Bales and Warner, p. 55.

"This, together, with the dismal prospect of future want, oblig'd me to keep a strict watch over the rest of the Body, least any of 'em shou'd (if able) get to it, and this being spent, we be forc'd to feed upon the living: which we must certainly have done, had we staid a few days longer." Bales and Warner, p. 35.

"Nor is there any more Truth in the Care which the Captain ascribes to himself, in hindring us to eat too much of the Corps lest it should prejudice our Health; for we all agreed, the Night before we come off; to limit our selves, . . ." Bales and Warner, p. 55.

"Langman, Mellen, and White reported that the castaways 'kept a great Fire, which was seen on Shore, and proved very comfortable to us, both for its Warmth, and by Broiling part of the Dead Corpse, which made it eat with less Disgust.'" Bales and Warner, p. 56.

"'I found (in a few days) their very natural dispositions chang'd,' he explained 'and that affectionate, peacable temper they had all along hitherto discover'd totally lost; their eyes staring and looking wild . . .'" and following. Bales and Warner, p. 35.

"Deane's opponents deny all this. Instead they say it was he who turned. It wasn't the members of the crew who lost their Christian temperance but the gentlemen from Nottinghamshire."

"All the Oaths we heard were between the Captain, his Brother and Mr. Whitworth, who often Quarrel'd about their Lying and Eating." and following. Bales and Warner, p. 55.

"Whereas the Captain often went to Prayers with us before we had the Corps to eat, he never, to our hearing, pray'd afterwards, but behav'd himself so impiously, that he was many times rebuked by the Mate and others for Profane Swearing." Bales and Warner, p. 55.

CHAPTER **14**

"According to the deponents he 'had not the Face to deny it, his Character appeared in a True light, and he was covered with Shame and Confusion.'" Bales and Warner, p. 44.

"Captain Deane dated his *Narrative*, 'Boston, NE [New England], Jan 26, 1710,' which would have been just a few weeks after the ship's company landed at Portsmouth, but it was not until the beginning of March that Mather even acknowledged receiving it. 'A remarkable Relation of Distress undergone a Deliverance received by some Sea-faring People is putt into my Hands,' he wrote in his diary on March 4." *Diary of Cotton Mather,* Winter 1710–1711 to Spring 1711, March 4, 1711.

"All of this might have distracted Mather from publishing the captain's account of the *Nottingham Galley* shipwreck. But maybe, too, the depositions left by the captain's opponents made the moralist in him think twice." *Diary of Cotton Mather,* Winter 1710–1711 to Spring 1711.

"On January 22, the *Boston News Letter* reported that 'hard weather by Frost, Snow and Thaw hindered the posts' . . ." *Boston News Letter,* January 28, 1711, February 18–25, 1711, and March 26, 1711.

"Meanwhile search-and-destroy missions were being dispatched to hunt down native inhabitants." and following. *Boston News Letter* January 28, 1711, February 18–25, 1711, and March 26 1711.

"St. George's River to drive the Indians from fishing & fowling which is their support this season of the year." *Boston News Letter,* March 26, 1711.

"Many failed to retain the 'perfect use' of their arms and legs. When spring came at last, several of the *Nottingham Galley* mariners answered the call of the sea once again, taking up the invitation to work on local ships, 'some sailing one way and some another,' remembered a cheerful Captain Deane." Bales and Warner, pp. 38–39.

"The point was 'to make a Good Use of much Evil occurring in the World, and especially of the strange Punishments inflicted by God on many sinners in the World, and most especially of the Things befalling the Sea-faring Tribe.'" *Cotton Mather Diary*, May 6, 1711.

"A large middle class of artisans and shopkeepers bridged the two Londons, adding necessary social cohesion and charting a difficult though not impossible route to social advancement." Trevelyan, George Macauley. *The England of Queen Anne, Vol. I.* London: Green and Co., 1934, pp. 72–82; Porter, Roy. *London: A Social History.* London: Hamish Hamilton, 1994, pp. 157–193.

"Phrases like 'seeing the mercy of God in the midst of Judgment' and any references to psalm singing were absent . . ." Deane Narrative (Mather, ed. January 1710–1711).

"One of the men went out on the Boltsprint, and returning, told me he saw something black ahead, and wou'd adventure to get on shore, accompanied with any other Person; upon which I desir'd some of the best swimmers (My Mate and one more) to go with him, and if they recover'd the Rock, to give notice by their Calls, and direct us to the most secure Place." Bales and Warner, p. 25.

"Langman later denied this anecdote, noting that he didn't even know how to swim." Bales and Warner, p. 50.

"If 'Mr. Whitworth, a young Gentleman, his Mother's darling Son, delicately educated' amid 'great an Affluence' could suggest eating the Carpenter, then their circumstances were surely dire enough to countenance something so ghastly." Bales and Warner, pp. 80–81.

"Captain Deane recorded in this later addition of his *Narrative* that he passively listened to the arguments and pleadings of his fellow castaways with an 'invincible Silence,' and he claims that he was only brought to the gruesome task after the others prevailed upon him with 'incessant Prayers and Tears.'" Bales and Warner, pp. 80–81.

"'Two of us did positively refuse it in publick Company,' Langman, Mellen, and White said, 'after reading a part of it, and told him to his Face that it was not true.'" Bales and Warner, p. 43.

"Since Portsmouth the trio had 'Apprehensions' that John Deane might misrepresent matters when they were all back in London. It squared with his character, which is why, they contend, they had refused 'the Encouragement which was offered to us in New England,' unlike some of the others." Bales and Warner, p. 43.

CHAPTER 15

"Once again they swore under oath that their statements were the truth, made copies, and, according to the Deane brothers and Miles Whitworth, 'industriously spread abroad' the depositions." Bales and Warner, p. 39.

"A crowd of idle pamphlets." Markman Ellis, *The Coffee House: A Cultural History*. London: Weidenfeld & Nicolson, 2004; Brian Cowan, *The Social Life of Coffee: The Emergence of the British Coffee House*. Yale University Press, 2005; and Straus.

Beyond the common characteristics of hot beverages and a table containing literature, coffeehouses became specialized." and following information on London's coffeehouse scene. Markman, Cowan, and Straus.

"The business continued right into the coffeehouses, located in Exchange Alley, or on Lombard Street, where agreements were made and auctions held 'by inch of candle.'" When the inch of candle burned out, the bidding on any particular item ended.

"The London court of public opinion that would try the case of Captain John Deane essentially encompassed these few blocks." Ellis, p. 166.

"In 1673, letters from common seamen critical of their officers found their way onto literature tables after an indecisive battle at sea, embarrassing the government." Ellis, p. 89.

"About ten days later a classified advertisement appeared in the *London Gazette*, which announced 'this day is published, *A Narrative of the Sufferings, Preservation and Deliverance of Capt. John Deane and Company in the Nottingham Galley of London, cast away on Boon Island near New England, December 11, 1710.*'" *London Gazette*, August 11, 1711.

"At one point Langman, Mellen, and White noted that of their three opponents—the Deane brothers and Whitworth—only John Deane was 'acquainted with all the Matter of Fact' during their travails." Bales and Warner, p. 44.

"They were part of group of associates who included the well-known John Dunton, at times a 'publisher, whole sale, retail and 2nd hand bookseller, auctioneer, journalist and hack.'" Parks, Stephen. *John Dunton and the English Book Trade: A Study of His Career with a Checklist of His Publications*. New York: Garland Publishing, 1976, p. 5.

"Published in pamphlet form the new *Narrative* was distributed throughout London via hawkers or 'mercury traders,' men and women who sold printed material on the streets and in the coffee circuit." and the following information about the mercury traders. Paula McDowell, "Women in the London Book Trade" in *The Women of Grub Street: Press, Politics and Gender in the London Marketplace, 1678–1730*. Oxford: Clarendon Press, 1998, pp. 58–59, 84–85.

"In their postscript the Deanes declared, 'Having two or three spare Pages, we think it our duty to the truth, and our selves, to obviate a barbarous and scandalous Reflection, industriously spread abroad and level'd at our ruine, by some unworthy, Malicious Persons.'" Bales and Warner, p. 39.

"Women had a long history in the stationer's trades—nuns had labored at the Ripoli Monestary Press in Florence near the advent of printing, and the first copies of the American Declaration of Independence were printed by a woman, Mary Catherine Goddard." Hudak, Leona M. *Early American Women Printers and Publishers, 1639–1820*. London: The Scarecrow Press, 1978, p. 2.

In England in 1711, 7 percent of all printers or stationers were women, and there were probably more, as many women who may have in practice acted the part of principle printer, were hidden behind their husbands' or fathers' names." Barker, Hannah and Chalus, Ellen. *Gender in 18th Century England: Roles, Representations and Responsibilities*. Harlow: Longman, 1997, pp. 81–100.

"Most who came to own printing or bookselling businesses did so through male family members, though 108 women entered the trade through apprenticeships between 1666 and 1800." McDowell, p. 35.

"She knew how to work the system, and in the case of the unfolding *Nottingham Galley* story, she likely saw an opportunity." Parks, p. 5; McDowell, pp. 42–45. Plomber, Henry, Ed. *A Dictionary of the Printers and Booksellers Who Were at Work in England, Scotland and Ireland from 1688 to 1725*. London: Bibliographical Society, 1907.

"It has been suggested this was an unauthorized version, but the bit about 'casting of Lots' printed on the cover seems to be the only significant change from the original full Jasper Deane–edited version. Warner, p. 7. There is no price or specific date of publication on *A Sad and Deplorable but True Account*, printed by J. Dunton, 1711.

"The financially struggling Dunton probably printed this shorter version of the story in order to cash in on the sensation, a story, Dunton wrote, 'very well known by most merchants on the *Royal Exchange*.'" John Dunton, writing on the cover of A *Sad and Deplorable, but True*

Account of the Terrible Hardships and Suffering of Capt. John Deane & Company on Board the Nottingham Galley, London: J. Dunton, 1711.

"Deane's *Narrative* was 'printed by R. Tooke' and 'sold by S. Popping,' while Langman, Mellen, and White's Account was 'printed for S. Popping.'"

CHAPTER 16

"Jasper Deane wrote, 'And for the Satisfaction of others, I would only need offer, that both his Character and my own may be easily gain'd by Enquiry.'" Bales and Warner, p. 23.

"'Likewise,' continued Jasper Deane, 'several of his [John Deane's] Fellow Sufferers being now in Town, their Attestations might be procur'd, if saw a real Necessity.'" Bales and Warner, p. 23.

"It was the first point they made in the introduction of their Account, referring to the claim as a 'Notorious Falsehood.'" Bales and Warner, p. 43.

"In so doing they gave themselves credibility by honoring that social order, even identifying themselves as 'only sailors,' and thus acknowledging their inferior place on its ladder." Bales and Warner, p. 44.

"The trio closed out their introduction with, 'And since what we deliver is upon Oath, we hope it will obtain Credit sooner than the bare Word of Captain Deane, his brother, and Mr. Whitworth, who were all three interested persons . . .'" Bales and Warner, p. 44.

"He did mention his two 'honored Friends,' the leading gentlemen of Portsmouth, New Hampshire, John Wentworth and John Plaisted, but Deane was obliged to thank these men and, to refer to them as 'Friends', was to use their social status and reputations to serve his own." Bales and Warner, p. 38.

"As the captain noted: 'Twas more than Ten Thousand to one but every man had perish'd.'" Bales and Warner, pp. 39–40.

"Their new position appeared as part of the very lengthy title of their *Account*, where they stated that the ship was lost 'by the Captain's obstinacy.'" The full title of Langman, Mellen, and White's *Account* is *A True Account of the Voyage of the* Nottingham-Galley *of London, John Dean Commander, from the River Thames to New-England, Near which place she was cast away on Boon-Island, December 11, 1710 by the Captain's Obstinacy, who endeavour'd to betray her to the French, or run her ashore; with an account of the falsehoods in the Captain's Narrative. And a faithful Relation of the Extremities the Company was reduc'd to for Twenty-four Days on that desolate Rock, where they were forc'd to eat one of their Companions who died, but were at last wonderfully deliver'd.*

"In their revised *Narrative*, for the first time, the brothers acknowledged 'being chas'd by two large Privateers, in their Passage Northabout to Killybegs.'" Bales and Warner, p. 39.

"And they challenged anyone with knowledge of them—or another investor in the ship—taking out more insurance than £250 between England and Ireland, or £300 pounds between Ireland and New England . . ." Bales and Warner, p. 40.

"And Now, let the Word judge whether 'tis reasonable to imagine we shou'd willfully lose a Ship of 120 Tuns, besides a valuable Interest in Cargo in such a Place, where the Commander (as well as the Rest) must unavoidably run the utmost Hazard of perishing in the most miserable Manner, and all this to recover £226 17s how absurd and ridiculous is such a Supposition, and yet this is the Reproach we at present labor under, so far as to receive daily ignominious Scandals upon our Reputations, and injurious Affronts and Mobbings to our Faces." Bales and Warner, p. 40.

CHAPTER **17**

"The first mate said 'The Day following they saw the Privateers again, when the said John Deane (contrary to the Will of this Deponent) would have brought the Ship *Nottingham* to an Anchor, which if done, she would in all probability have been taken.'" Bales and Warner, pp. 61–62.

"By the time the three disaffected seamen got around to writing their *Account,* the individual opinions had been discussed at length, shared with others, and clarified, so that they could finally conclude that Captain Deane lost the ship through 'obstinacy' on the night of the storm, and earlier 'endeavour'd to betray her [the Nottingham Galley] to the French, or run her ashore.'" See title of Langman, Mellen, and White's *Account.*

"When they finally got around to discussing the encounter with the French privateers, the Deane brothers claimed that as a last resort, if there were no means of escape, they would, as they discussed aboard the *Nottingham Galley,* 'run the Ship on Shore *and burn her.*'" Bales and Warner, p. 39.

"It was said that a 'Great trade' was 'carried on with France from Dublin, Waterford, Ross, Cork and Lymrick.'" *Journal of the English House of Lords,* Vol. 17, March 1, 1705.

"In April last, going between Olerone and St. Martin, they met Six Sail of English and Irish vessels, coming out among many *French* ships; and One Ketch coming near the Ship in which Captain Fowles was on, he asked, 'Whither they were bound?' And they answering, 'For Ireland.'" *Journal of the English House of Lords,* Vol. 17, March 1, 1705.

"He saw Wm. Williamson taking an Account of Provisions then landing out of a Pink; which, Williamson told him, belonged to Alderman Bell of Dublin. He also said, There were Fifteen English and Irish Ships in the Port, who waited to go out with several Ships of War that lay in the Road, and were reported to be victualed, and some of them loaden with Provisions out of those Ships." *Journal of the English House of Lords,* Vol. 17, 1 March 1705.

"Four years later, in 1708, he published pamphlets about the ongoing problem, which had only gotten worse." TK (Thomas Knox). "A Brief Account of the Woolen Manufacturing of England with Relation to the Prejudices it Receives By the Clandestine Exportation of Wool from Ireland into France." London: Printed and sold by A. Baldwin, 1708.

"'Though 'tis prohibited by an Act of parliament [trade with France],' wrote RF, 'we find a surreptitious Trade continually carrying on thither, in contempt of the same . . .'" RF. *An Enquiry into the Causes of the Prohibition of Commerce with France . . . with an Account of the fraudulent Methods usually taken to cheat her Majesty of her Customs.* London: B. Braggs, 1708.

"According to Knox, Irish products, especially wool, were disguised as barrels of beef and 'conveyed into Creeks or Islands.'" TK (Thomas Knox).

"RF wrote tellingly, 'By sham Captures, what gross Cheats and Abuses are the Work of every Day, are numberless; *viz* by taking ships freighted with Wine and Brandy, by private Contract and Assignation: By Seizures being made by the Importers own Information, after private Agreement and Bonds enter'd into between him and the Seizor.'" RF.

"Could this be what Captain Deane and his associates were up to when First Mate Langman stopped them?" TK (Thomas Knox).

"Knox noted before Parliament that the trade between the two nations was not only about wool and wine, but that '*French* Fleets, Privateers and Plantations [were] furnished with provisions by this Traffick.'" *Journal of the English House of Lords,* Volume 17, March 1, 1705.

"(Members of Rogers's crew, hungry for plunder, were unconvinced of the Swedish ship's innocence and had to be disciplined for mutinous behavior after the potential prize was released.)" Rogers, Woodes. *Privateer—Life aboard a British Privateer in the Time of Queen Anne, 1708–1711*. Paean Books, 2011, pp. 17–18.

"In the French port of St. Malo there was a 'persistent demand for the building of ships and houses and for the feeding of an inflated wartime population' wrote historian J. S. Bromley." Bromley, J. S. *Corsairs and Navies, 1660–1760*. London: The Hambledan Press, 1987.

"As an illustration of the constant and often urgent need for cordage, an English diplomat once remarked that if a certain convoy carrying hemp from Russia 'should by accident Miscary, it will be impossible for His Majesty to fit out any ships of war for the next year, by which means the whole navy of England will be rendered perfectly useless.'" The British Ambassador at the Hague to Lord Stafford, quoted in Lisk, Jill. *The Struggle for Superiority in the Baltic, 1600–1725*. London: University of London Press, 1967, p. 23.

"An English frigate of the period might have one quarter of its hold packed with extra cordage at the beginning of a voyage." Leslie, Robert, ed. *Robert Leslie in Life Aboard a British Privateer in the Time of Queen Anne: Being the Journal of Captain Woodes Rogers, Master Mariner*. London: Chapman and Hall, 1889, p. 9.

"Convoys were very regular to the southern coast of Ireland, and in that area English merchant shipping had the added protection of five to eight English warships, which were on permanent station to deter an invasion of Ireland and prosecute smuggling." Hattendorf, John. *England in the War of Spanish Succession: A Study of the English View and Conduct of Grand Strategy, 1701–1713*. New York: Garland, 1987, pp. 168–171.

"Captain Deane, however, ordered the *Nottingham Galley* to northern Ireland, where there was virtually no chance of encountering an English warship, and where buying cheese to sell in Boston, or anywhere else, would be much more difficult." O'Donovan, John. *The Economic History of Live Stock in Ireland.* Cork: University of Cork Press, 1940.

"It's not unreasonable to assume that they were stuck in Killybegs for forty-two days because they couldn't find a cargo fit for Boston, France, or both, in such a remote corner." Killybegs was known for fish—but so was New England.

"The man's heroic character is never questioned by Langman, Mellen, and White, but in their version he is not a Swede, but instead a 'stout Dutchman.'" Bales and Warner, p. 53.

"England's Dutch allies traded with France throughout the war, and at times that commerce included naval stores." For evidence of Scandinavian and Dutch wartime trade in naval stores with France, see Bromley, J. S. "La France de l'Ouest et la Guerre Maritime" in *Corsairs and Navies.* London: Hambleton, 1987, pp. 394–395.

"Or perhaps he was born earlier, estranged from his father, or illegitimate, and only reconciled by 1710." This scenario is supported by the births of a Charles Whitworth born in 1688 and presumably a sister, Mary, born in 1685, both in Whittlebury, England. Two of the deceased Mile Whitworth's children were named Charles and Mary. Charles later took the name Miles.

"In the conclusion to their story, Langman, Mellen, and White declared, 'All this we Avouch to be Truth' and have no other End in publishing it, but to testify our Thankfulness to God for his Great Deliverance, and to give others Warning not to trust their Lives or Estates in the hands of so wicked and brutish a Man [as Captain John Deane].'" Bales and Warner, p. 58.

CHAPTER **18**

"The captain's brother faced Langman, raised the bottle, and 'struck him' with it, surprising him with the blow." Bales and Warner, p. 47.

"Seconds later the captain reappeared up out of the hold. But rather than water for the men, he had a club in his hand, a 'Periwig Block,' a wooden stand 'such as Barbers make Wigs on.'" Bales and Warner, p. 47.

"'We all thought that he had kill'd him,' remembered Boatswain Nicholas Mellen and Seaman George White, 'for he lay dead some time, and lost a great deal of Blood.'" Bales and Warner, p. 141.

"Langman lay there on the deck bleeding out—it was a severe beating—but in the annals of the sea such a thrashing was certainly not unheard of." and the following paragraph. Rediker, p. 217.

"In addition to the usual sticks and canes, sailors report to have received blows to the head with a stone mug, a bull's foot, a 'Manyrocker, (which is a tough Root as thick as a Man's Legg),' and even 'an Elephant's dry'd Pizle.'" Pizle: Penis. Rediker, pp. 216–217.

"But Captain Deane himself refers to fleeing the sinking *Nottingham Galley* with neither 'wig nor cap.'" Bales and Warner, p. 68.

"The case made by Langman, Mellen, and White against Captain Deane contrasts with instances in which sea captains are clearly sadistic, . . ." See Druett, Joan. *In the Wake of Madness: The Murderous Voyage of the Whaleship Sharon*. Chapel Hill: Algonquin Books, 2004.

"Langman, Mellen, and White don't say how long the first mate lay on the deck bleeding as the clouds darkened around them, but they do say the sight of him was 'very discouraging to the Seamen, who durst not speak to him for fear of the like treatment.'" Bales and Warner, p. 48.

"Because of the overcast skies, they'd had difficulty accurately gauging their position, and many aboard 'Perceiv'd the ship in Danger by being so near land.'" Bales and Warner, p. 48.

"'Scarce recovered,' remembered Mellen, the first mate was still covered in his own blood." Bales and Warner, p. 48.

"Langman said he told Deane that 'he had no Business so near Land, except he had a Mind to lose the Ship, and therefore desir'd him to hawl further off, or else he would be ashore that Night.' At this, Deane flew into a rage. He told Langman 'he wou'd not take his Advice though the Ship should go to the Bottom.'" Bales and Warner, p. 48.

"Instead of following the Mate's wiser tack, the captain pulled out a pistol, and 'threatened to shoot the Mate.'" Bales and Warner, p. 48.

"In the first version of his *Narrative*, the captain reports the ship heading 'something southerly.'" Deane, Mather edition, 1710–1711.

"In the second version he has the ship 'haling Southerly for the Massachusetts-Bay, under a hard gale of Wind at North-East.'" Bales and Warner, p. 24.

"By the time Deane got around to revising his Narrative in 1726, sixteen years after the fact, he changed his story, saying since 'the Wind being N.E. and the Land lying N.E and S.W, they concluded it both Safe and Advisable to steer S.W. 'till 10 a Clock at Night and then lie by 'till Morning, with the Head of their Vessel off from Land.'" Bales and Warner, p. 66.

"First Mate Langman was recuperating from his injury—Deane referred to him as 'indisposed'; the trio referred to him as 'still in his cabin, and hardly done bleeding'—and was unable to perform his duty." Bales and Warner, p. 67.

For Langman, Mellen, and White's account of the shipwreck and the captain's behavior thereafter, see Bales and Warner, pp. 48–50. All quotes about the event are derived from that source.

"Deane, in his *Narrative*, suggested his own conduct at that critical moment was calm and collected, especially compared to members of his crew, who all but collapsed. But in the account of the three sailors, Captain Deane panics, becoming hysterical. In a crisis, 10 to 15 percent of all people experience a high degree of such behavior, including 'uncontrolled weeping, confusion, screaming, and paralyzing anxiety.'" Leach. pp. 22–31.

Epilogue

"John Deane's eleven years in Russia are shrouded in even more mystery than the rest of his life . . ." There is apparently a significant number of records pertaining to John Deane in the Russian Naval Archives in St. Petersburg. What is known of this material, and most of the information described here regarding Deane's career in Russia, comes from historian Richard H. Warner, who at the time of this writing, was working on a full biography of John Deane. See Warner's essay in Roberts, pp. 3–17.

Deane later recorded that the ship, 'after careening and repairing, sailed from Archangel, and passing the North Cape [of Norway] the last of November, with much ado got in and wintered about 25 leagues from Trondhjem, losing much of her crew through the asperity of this cold season.'" Deane, John. *A History of the Russian Fleet During the Reign of Peter the Great*, Bridge, Cyprian G., ed. London: Navy Records Society, 1899, pp. 44–45. The authorship of *A History of the Russian Fleet During the Time of Peter the Great* was only discovered in the 1930s, and was revealed in *Mariners' Mirror*, July 20, 1934, p. 373.

"Returning home Deane tried his hand at letters again. He sought to capitalize on his long experience in Russia by producing a document, 'A History of the Russian Fleet during the Reign of Peter the Great,'

which he hoped would be useful to the English Crown." and the following paragraph. Deane, John. *A History of the Russian Fleet During the Reign of Peter the Great.*

"Tilson interviewed Deane and wrote to his boss, 'Captain Deanee undertook to be useful to us and showed us a letter from Admiral Apraksin, who seems to be a power in that country [Russia], which persuaded us he might render service.'" and other Tilson quotes from "George Tillson to Lord Townsend," letters quoted in Warner, p. 9.

"The post was only 'colour,' wrote Tilson, 'but his true business is to transmit hither what intelligence he may be able to get for His Majesty's service.'" George Tillson to Lord Townsend, quoted in Warner, p. 9.

"Informing the English diplomat Stephen Poyntz of Deane's mission, Townsend prefaced his note cryptically, saying 'You know John Deane as well as I do, I take him to be an honest man.'" Lord Townsend to Stephen Poyntz, quoted in Chance, James Frederick. *The Alliance of Hanover: A Study of British Foreign Policy in the Last Years of George I.* London: John Murray, 1923, p. 84.

"Sir Nathanial Gould, on behalf of the English Russian Company, had urged against sending Deane because he was 'very prejudicial to our mercantile affairs,' and 'very obnoxious' to the Russian government." Chance, p. 107.

"Deane reminded Tilson that he'd only accepted the mission to Russia 'with great reluctance, having formerly experienced the malice of that sett of men, but it was impossible for any person not present to believe with what bitterness they had persecuted me in Russia.'" and following quotes in the paragraph. John Deane to George Tilson, August 25, 1725.

"'I make no doubt,' Deane stated, 'but my adversary has found means . . . of Representing me a Monster in Nature.'" John Deane to George Tilson, July 5, 1725.

"**Feeble on Boon Island, powerless in St. Petersburg, John Deane now moved a nation.**" Fritz, Paul. *The English Ministers and Jacobism between the Rebellions of 1715 and 1745.* University of Toronto Press. 1975.

"**Local tradition has it that John and Jasper Deane had parted on bad terms when John Deane left for St. Petersburg in 1711.**" Some of the folklore, however, is unsupported by the surviving documentation. It is said that Jasper Deane was a doctor, but his will, when he took it out, has him as a "mariner." When he died and the will was executed, he was described as a farmer. At no time on Boon Island, when medical knowledge was in demand, was Jasper Deane ever mentioned as making a contribution.

"**That's the folklore, and indeed, Jasper Deane died in 1726, the year of his brother's return home, leaving an estate of £73, including twenty-two sheep, two pigs, one calf, and £35 in real estate.**" Inventory of Jasper Deane, Public Records, Nottinghamshire, England.

"'**As, after a shipwreck,' declared Deane, 'all Discipline and Command ceases, and all are reduc'd to a State of Equality; so that late Master [Deane himself] perceiving some refusing to give Assistance even when required in necessary Matters, he purposefully withdrew from the Society under the Pretense of collecting Materials for future Use, in order to give them a fair Opportunity of freely electing a Head, or Chief Commander.'**" and following quotes. Bales and Warner, p. 70.

"**Extraordinarily, even in death, John Deane found the means to carry on his lifelong battle against his enemies. In his will his wife Sarah would have received the support from the estate she brought into the marriage, and Deane's very elderly half sister was to get an annuity.**" *Last Will and Testament,* John Deane of Wilford, executed July 23, 1762, Records of the Prerogative Court of Canterbury, PRO PROB 11/882.

Mary Lorring was to apply the money for "the use and maintenance of herself and her family and not embezel or waist it in fruitless and unnecessary expenses upon her own person." Furthermore, Mary Lorring and her family were not to give John Deane's wife or trustees "any Insult or trouble on their account and that the said Edward Lorring and said wife Mary or their children shall not reside or rome within forty miles of my said wife." If they did, then Sarah Deane and the other trustees had the right to cut off their inheritance. *Last Will and Testament,* John Deane of Wilford, executed 23 July 1762, Records of the Prerogative Court of Canterbury, PRO PROB 11/882.

"**Three hundred years later, and the captain's story continues to be heard. Captain Deane's** *Narrative* **has been published three times since his death, in 1917, 1968, and 1996.**" William Abbatt republished the Jasper Deane edited version in the *Magazine of History and Biography with Notes and Queries,* Vol. 59 (1917), pp. 199–217. Mason Phillip Smith republished the same versions in *A Narrative of the Shipwreck of the* Nottingham Galley, *in her Voyage from England to Boston, with an Account of the Miraculous Escape of the Captain and his Crew, etc.* (Portland, Maine: Provincial Press. 1968). Most thoroughly, Richard Warner and Jack Bales include two versions of Captain Deane's *Narrative,* and all of the Langman, Mellen, and White documents, including their *Account* in the republication of Kenneth Robert's *Boon Island* (Hanover, NH: University Press of New England. 1996.) Warner does not include the first version of Deane's *Narrative,* edited by Cotton Mather, and he gets the chronology of Deane's various versions wrong by claiming that the Mather edition followed the Jasper Deane edition, when in fact it preceded it and was penned by Deane in the days immediately following his rescue.

"**In all of this literature, the dissenting point of view Langman, Mellen, and White is sometimes acknowledged but never thoroughly considered.**" See Thomas, R. *Remarkable Shipwrecks, Fires, Famines and Calamities, Providential Deliverances, and Lamentable Disasters at Sea* (Hartford: Andrus, 1835); Barrington, George. *Remarkable Voyages and*

Shipwrecks etc. (London: Simpkin, Marshall, Hamilton & Kent, 1881); Snow, Edward Rowe, ed. *Great Storms and Famous Shipwrecks of the New England Coast* (Boston: Yankee, 1943); Paine, Ralph D., ed. *Lost Ships and Lonely Seas.* (New York: Century, 1921); and Huntress, Keith. *Narratives of Shipwrecks and Disasters at Sea* (1974). Huntress mistakenly names the ships' boy "Mosses Butler," which was the fictional name given to him by Kenneth Roberts.

"Kingston treats the Boon Island episode as an unrecognizable afterthought, in which the ship wrecks not in the winter off New England . . ." Kingston, William Henry Giles. *John Deane of Nottingham.* Available widely as a free ebook.

"His biographer, Jack Bales, noted, 'While Roberts had the journalist ability to research his articles, he seldom viewed any issue from more than one perspective, and rarely scrutinized the data to find the significance of the facts he had uncovered.'" Bales, Jack. *Kenneth Roberts.* New York: Twayne Publishers, 1993, p. 31.

"When interviewed about Boon Island, Roberts said of Langman that he 'accused Deane of all sorts of impossible things.'" and following. Nichols, Lewis. "A Visit with Mr. Roberts," *New York Times,* January 1, 1956, quoted in Bales. *Kenneth Roberts,* p. 13.

"In his early days as a journalist, Roberts made a name for himself at the *Saturday Evening Post,* where he carried the banner of nativism—the author was rabidly antiimmigrant." "If the United States is the melting pot," railed Roberts, "something is wrong with the heating system; for an inconveniently large portion of the new immigration floats round in unsightly indigestible lumps. Of recent years the contents of the melting pot have stood badly in need of straining, in order that the refuse might be removed and deposited in the customary receptacle for such things." Quoted in Bales. *Kenneth Roberts,* p. 14.

INDEX

About the Authors

Andrew Vietze is an award-winning writer from Maine. The former managing editor of *Down East: The Magazine of Maine*, he's the author of six previous books, including the critically acclaimed *Becoming Teddy Roosevelt*, and has written for a wide array of print and online publications, from *Time Out New York* to Weather.com, the *New York Times' LifeWire* to *Offshore*. A registered Maine guide, he works as a seasonal ranger in one of the premier wilderness areas in the east. He's currently at work on a memoir about life as a park ranger, and a thriller about the North Woods during the lumber camp era. Find out more at andrewvietze.com.

Stephen Erickson holds master's in American history from the University of Massachusetts at Amherst and completed coursework on a doctorate in early American history from the College of William and Mary. He frequently draws on his background in American history as a political reformer. Erickson is currently the president of Americans United to Rebuild Democracy.